Bible
Highways

BOOKS BY IVOR POWELL

BIBLE CAMEOS
These eighty graphic "thumb-nail" sketches are brief biographies of Bible people. Pungent and thought-provoking studies.

BIBLE HIGHWAYS
In this series of Bible studies, Scripture texts are linked together, suggesting highways through the Bible from Genesis to Revelation.

BIBLE PINNACLES
A spiritual adventure into the lives and miracles of Bible characters and the meaningful parables of our Lord.

BIBLE TREASURES
In refreshingly different style and presentation, these eighty Bible miracles and parables are vividly portrayed.

BIBLE WINDOWS
Anecodotes and stories are, in fact, windows through which the Gospel light shines, to illumine lessons for teachers and preachers.

MARK'S SUPERB GOSPEL
This most systematic study offers expositional, devotional and homiletical thoughts. The enrichment gained from the alliteration outlines will create a desire for more truth.

LUKE'S THRILLING GOSPEL
In this practical and perceptive commentary, there is a goldmine of expository notes and homilies.

JOHN'S WONDERFUL GOSPEL
Another verse-by-verse distinctively different commentary with sermonic notes and outlines.

WHAT IN THE WORLD WILL HAPPEN NEXT?
An unusual work on prophecy dealing especially with the return of Christ to earth and the nation of Israel's future.

Bible
Highways

by

Ivor Powell

Foreword by

Wilfred L. Jarvis

KREGEL PUBLICATIONS
Grand Rapids, Michigan 49501

Bible Highways by Ivor Powell. Copyright © 1959
by Ivor Powell. Published 1985 by Kregel Publications,
a division of Kregel, Inc. All rights reserved.

Library of Congress Cataloging in Publication Data

Powell, Ivor, 1910-
   Bible Highways.

Reprint. Originally published: London: Marshall,
Morgan & Scott, 1959.
   1. Bible—Meditations. I. Title.
BS491.5.P68 1985   220.6   85-8097
ISBN 0-8254-3521-8

Printed in the United States of America

CONTENTS

INDEX OF ILLUSTRATION

FOREWORD

It is with a deep sense of privilege that I write this fore-word to the Rev. Ivor Powell's latest book, *Bible Highways*. For two years Mr. Powell has conducted evangelistic missions across Canada under the auspices of the Baptist Federation of Canada. He quickly established a reputation as a gifted expositor and an evangelist of impassioned zeal, balanced by a fine sanity of utterance and technique. He possesses a rare gift for making the Bible "live" for his hearers—a gift which is equally demonstrated in his numerous writings. To a generation suffering from neglect of the Scriptures as the Word of life, Mr. Powell is rendering salutary service through his books with their blend of traditional canons of interpretation and of incisive, vivid, contemporary application.

I hope that this volume will reach the hands of a great host of readers—especially those of a new generation of Christians. It will contribute to an exciting discovery of the wonder of the inspired Word, and to a renewed confidence in its relevance to human life with all its sin, complexity, confusion, yearning, hope, and glorious potentialities under God.

Canadian Baptists cannot avoid a sense of satisfaction in the fact that this book has been written in Canada, and the hope that Mr. Powell's years amongst us may have contributed something to his insight into the sufficiency of the Gospel for sinful men.

General Secretary-Treasurer,   THOMAS B. McDORMAND
Baptist Federation of Canada
Toronto, Ontario

PREFACE

This book has been written because public demand asked for a volume a little different from its predecessors. Earlier readers will know that the initial Bible volumes of this series supplied studies planned to help young ministers and others in the preparation of their addresses. *Bible Windows* supplemented these with suitable illustrations of many kinds. I am grateful for the favourable comments which came from many parts of the world, and there is reason to believe the books succeeded in fulfilling their mission. The suggestion has now been made that it would be of great worth if studies and illustrations could be combined in one volume, and it was this idea which gave birth to *Bible Highways*.

Within the pages of this book Bible studies and illustrations will alternate, for each exposition is followed by one or more stories which shed light on the theme already discussed. The name *Highways* was chosen because many of the studies suggest broad highways through the entire Bible. Texts are linked together to form a chain, and thus within the scope of one sermon readers may be transported in thought through centuries. It is not too much to suggest that ministers may find sufficient material in one message to last for two or even three addresses. It might be to their advantage to divide the study; but that, I trust, will be one of the delightful discoveries readers will make as they explore the following pages. I have enjoyed the production of this volume, and my sincere thanks are offered to the people who from time to time provided illustrations to be included in the collection.

I am grateful also to Dr. T. B. McDormand, who graciously wrote the Foreword. Throughout my stay in Canada, this untiring leader of the Baptist Federation was an unfailing friend. His winsome personality and unceasing enthusiasm for the cause of evangelism greatly encouraged me as I crusaded for Christ within the churches of the Federation. Dr. McDormand, and Dr. P. P. Ziemann of the Baptist House, Toronto, through whose instrumentality I first went to Canada, were my constant friends and advisers throughout the entire itinerary. For their fellowship I shall always thank God.

Bible Highways is now sent forth with the prayer that it might bring enjoyment to all who recognise the Scriptures to be the wonderful Word of God.

IVOR POWELL

THREE GARDENS . . . which tell their own stories

(GENESIS 2:8; JOHN 18:1; 19:41)

"And the Lord planted a garden eastward in Eden." I wish I could have seen that garden. Alas, I was born too late! Did it possess long winding paths, and were there enchanting borders of multi-coloured flowers? Were there shady corners where Adam sat listening to the songs of the birds? Were some of the flowering trees aflame with the Creator's art? And did the gentle breezes of evening produce music of exquisite sweetness as they played among the leaves? Yes, I wish I could have seen that garden, for it has been said, "One is nearer to God in a garden than anywhere else on earth." A garden is a mirror reflecting a world. There, we find enemies; there, we find friends. Within the confines of a garden stalks the shadow of death; but in that same shadow may be found promise of glorious resurrection. The gardens of the Bible have a wonderful story to tell.

The Garden of Tragedy . . . death commencing

It was all over, and poor Adam hardly knew where he was or what he was doing. Tears probably blinded his eyes, and a cloud on the sun sent shadows scurrying across the lawn. The time would now come when newly turned earth would announce an addition to the Creator's design. The day would eventually dawn when a grave would be found in God's wonderful world, and for a while the birds would cease to sing. Yes, it was now a certainty that some day human blood would stain the good earth: for Adam had sinned! For ever he would remember the sinister whisper which had said, "Ye shall not surely die." He frowned. Death was an unpleasant word. How could he die, when he had only just commenced to live? He shuddered as another cloud passed across his soul. He had not died physically; but his innocence, his purity, his joy had ceased to exist. Germs had invaded his soul, and the grave which some day would spoil God's countryside would only be the forerunner of myriads more. Evil had lifted an ugly head; storm-clouds loomed on the horizon; and when Adam was required to leave his lovely home, he realised he had lost more than would ever be regained.

The Garden of Testing . . . death challenged

Someone had planted another garden. It was still and serene, for night had covered it with a shadowy mantle. There is reason to believe that the moon shone from the

1

heavens, for men that night were able to see things at which even the angels veiled their faces. The Prince of Heaven, a Knight in the shining armour of purity, had come to challenge the monster which from Eden had stalked through God's great world. Everywhere, a trail of anguish had been left behind this raging enemy. Homes had been plunged into sorrow; hearts had been ruthlessly broken; young lives had been snapped as if they had been but tender twigs, and death had reigned supreme. The monster had been invincible, for its greatest ally, sin, had its fifth column in every challenging heart. Now the tyrant was to meet his match; this was destined to be a night of nights. There is hardly need to repeat what has been told elsewhere (*Bible Pinnacles,* p. 125); it is sufficient to say that although the Lord was hurt in the struggle, He succeeded in giving to His greatest enemy a fatal blow.

The Garden of Triumph . . . death conquered

The golden face of the sun was slowly appearing above the distant horizon; rays of scintillating brilliance were fast dispelling the shadows of the night. The silent garden was waking from sleep. Calm, dignified, radiant, an angel guarded the mouth of the sepulchre. His eyes were pools of happiness; the joy of the eternal shone from his face. When he saw the woman approaching, he smiled; he had great news to announce. " Be not affrighted: Ye seek Jesus of Nazareth, which was crucified: he is risen; he is not here: behold the place where they laid him. . . ." (Mark 16:6). I should love to have been in that garden. At the appointed time the stone was rolled away, and the King of Glory came forth triumphantly. Death had been vanquished—Eden's monster had been overcome, hope had been born anew. Now, forever God's children would be able to sing, " O death, where is thy sting? O grave, where is thy victory? "

It has been written that some day God will build a new world—and perhaps He will plant a new garden—*and there shall be no more death* (Rev. 21:4).

" Tell Me about My New Body

I met her in the garden alongside my church in Wales. Her children attended my Sunday-school, but I was disappointed when my efforts failed to attract the mother into the services. She came to the anniversaries when her youngsters took part, but I suspected she was not very happy in crowds. As I remember her now, I know my youthful inexperience failed to appreciate her problems. She was an abnormally stout woman, and was easily embarrassed. Yet I discovered hidden depths of spiritual wealth in that lady; deposits of true worth, the existence of which I never even suspected. I was working among the tulip beds one day, when she paused by the fence to express her appreciation of the way we had transformed waste land into a garden. As I listened to her, I began to realise that she also grew flowers—of another and rarer kind.

Months had passed; my friend was dying. I sat beside her bed, and was startled when she casually said, " Mr Powell, I'm dying. I know I haven't long to stay." Then in a whisper, as though she were trusting me with a great secret, she continued, " To tell you the truth, this old body has already started to die. My feet and my ankles have turned black, and the deadness is creeping up my legs. Oh yes, Mr. Powell, I'm dying; my old body was never much good, anyhow." Then she looked into my face and added, " Tell me about my new body—the one I'm going to have in heaven. Surely it will be far better than this old thing. Come, Mr. Powell, tell me about it."

I began to explain that the saints have bodies " like unto His glorious body," and reminded her that Christ retained His human body even after His resurrection—but it had been glorified. It was indeed the same body, for the marks of the nail-prints were still visible. Yet because it had been changed, locked doors were unable to prevent His entry into a room. I explained that His body was no longer sensitive to pain; that when He ascended into the sky, the laws of gravity were unable to pull Him back. His body would never age. I explained further that since angels were created before Adam, they were thousands of years old, and yet it was written of the angel who rolled away the stone from the tomb of Christ, *he was a young man.* Eternal bodies are ageless, insensitive to pain, glorious. Her face was shining; but when her daughter entered to ask a question, momentarily the radiance vanished. It seemed sacrilegious to speak of mundane matters after she had been hearing of eternal treasures. Quickly she answered the question, and then said, " Go on, Mr. Powell; you were saying about my new body. Tell me more." I told her all I knew, and after we had prayed together, left her supremely happy. Within a few days her mortal remains were lowered into a grave; but even as I watched, I knew " she was absent from the body and at home with the Lord." Within the garden of her soul she had produced blooms of rare beauty; she had already shared a resurrection of superlative worth.

The Underground Orchid

Western Australia is famous for wild flowers, and to be there in Springtime is to know an unforgettable experience. Much of the country appears to be desert, but a shower of rain performs miracles. A little moisture germinates the seeds, and soon the wild flowers cover the ground with a carpet of sheer loveliness. Then, most of the city people arrange trecks into the country to see these unrivalled gems of nature. The *Perth Daily Newspaper* Office has produced a book of " Australian Wild Flowers," and the colourful reproductions are a joy to behold. Toward the end of the book, reference has been made to the most famous of all the wild flowers—the underground orchid. This wonderful plant with its small purple flowers actually blossoms beneath the ground; its exquisite beauty is produced in the dark. At the time of my visit a complete specimen had not been obtained, for the only ones found had been brought to the surface and cut by the blades of a plough. It would hardly be permitted for naturalists to dig up thousands of acres in the hope of finding a complete orchid; yet it is now an ascertained fact that beneath the surface of the ground are little horticultural treasures the like of which the world has not known. They grow and blossom in the darkness. Their very existence was unsuspected, and only a great upheaval revealed the fact they were there.

This illustration perfectly expresses what I discovered in my friend of the garden. I did not realise that choice blooms lay hidden in her inner life. Possibly I should not have discovered these secrets if the rough blades of the ploughs of illness and circumstance had not thrown into bold relief the underground orchids of her soul.

> . . . One is nearer to God in a garden
> Than anywhere else on earth.

LIFE ETERNAL ... the most vital in the world

(GENESIS 2:9; JOHN 3:7; REVELATION 22:2)

Above us in outer space are innumerable planets, and their existence has aroused the interest of the entire world. Scholars study the night sky, and wonder what exists in the heavens. Are the planets inhabited? Will it be possible some day, with the aid of rocket ships, to explore the unknown? The Bible teaches that the heavens are the home of God, to which Christ and even the prophet Elijah ascended. It follows therefore that somewhere in the sky is the habitation of the great family of God. Death cannot be the termination of existence, but is rather the opening of a door to a greater experience—life eternal. The Bible has much to say in regard to this wondrous theme.

The Tree of Life in Eden

It should never be forgotten that *eternal life* is far greater than *everlasting life*. Eternal life is primarily something of quality. Everlasting life is something of duration—it never ends. Adam might have succeeded in living for ever—as mere man. He was meant to reach higher realms of experience— to share the nature of God; not merely to live endlessly, but to become a son of God by nature. Yet, man was not a robot, to be impelled by buttons or switches. Adam was given a free will. He was expected to exercise that gift, and thereby to demonstrate his fitness to share in the provision of his Maker. All this has been clearly revealed in the early chapters of Holy Writ. Man had to choose between the tree of life and the tree of knowledge of good and evil. The former was situated in the middle of the garden—the place of centrality, where its prominence invited attention; the latter tree was surrounded by God's prohibitions. When man permitted sin to stain his soul, the way to the tree of life was closed—" Lest man should put forth his hand, and take of the tree of life, and *live for ever*." Adam therefore lost his great opportunity, for sin had closed a highway.

The Tree of Life in John Three

I remember a man who complained, " It is not just. Why should I suffer because Adam sinned? It is not *my* fault that Adam went wrong. Why should God punish *me*? " This idea is false. When Christ discussed the topic with Nicodemus, He revealed that what had become an impossibility for Adam, was impossible no longer. He said, " Marvel not that I say unto you, ye must be born again." It was

5

possible for the Jewish leader to receive a new life—eternal life. This surely signifies that "the flaming sword" of Adam's day was now to be withdrawn. The question may be asked, How this could be; but the answer is unmistakable. The path to the tree of life was closed because of the existence of sin. If it is now to be reopened, it must be because the hindrance has been overcome. "For God so loved the world, that he gave his only begotten Son, that whosoever believeth in him should not perish, but have everlasting life." If Adam's sin robbed him of the power to choose eternal life, the death of Christ, by removing sin, restored what Adam lost. Once again man may choose unwisely; but at least *he can choose*. If man now suffers eternal loss, he does so, not because Adam went wrong, but because he has emulated Adam's example.

The Tree of Life in the New Jerusalem

In describing the new Jerusalem, John says, "In the midst of the street of it . . . was the tree of life . . . and the leaves of the tree were for the healing of the nations." It would seem that this verse presents a problem. Why should the nations need healing in the eternal kingdom? We have been led to believe that then all need will have been abolished. This verse harmonises with the rest of Scripture. When Christ returns to earth, He will reign for a thousand years, and afterwards, Satan will rally his forces to make a final onslaught on the powers of righteousness (Rev. 20:7-9). But not all men will follow evil. Many may desire to remain the subjects of the King of Kings. They will be ordinary humans, as we are; so how then can they share in the gift of God which enables men to live as God's children for ever? It would seem that the tree of life supplies the answer. Whether this be literal or symbolical is not of primary importance. The fact is that God makes it possible for people in all ages to *choose* life; and that always, man's destiny is decided by what he does when opportunity knocks at the door. God may offer the Bread of life, but unless man takes it he might easily die of starvation. "And the Spirit and the bride say, Come. And let him that heareth say, Come. And let him that is athirst come. And whosoever will, *let him take* the water of life freely" (Rev. 22:17).

Red Ribbons in Basutoland

South Africa is a great country. Undoubtedly political unrest is spoiling certain aspects of life for the various people who live there; undoubtedly many things could be changed for the betterment of the various races; undoubtedly much criticism may be levelled against the nation: but when all

6

has been said and done, Africa remains one of the greatest places in the world. I shall always thank God that He sent me to labour there for nearly four years. The native people are strange, and it was hard to escape the belief that although in some senses they seemed to be very primitive, there were many ways in which their innate wisdom surpassed that of the white man. I found cause for amazement and mirth in many of the antics of the untutored black people; similarly, they laughed loud and long at some of the things I tried—and failed—to do. The native peoples of South Africa charmed me. To sit with them around a camp fire, as I sometimes did; to listen to their strange tales; to examine their customs and beliefs, was an education. Whilst my wife collected the stamps of Basutoland, Swaziland, and Bechuanaland, I went in search of stories and customs. Some of these I shall never forget.

The story is told of a man who was passing through a village in Basutoland. Accustomed as he was to strange sights, he was nevertheless intrigued to see certain prized chickens walking about with bows of bright red ribbon tied under their wings and across their backs. This was something new. Other scraggy chickens were not so decorated; but a few enquiries revealed the fact that the native owner was always looking for red ribbon. When the man asked the owner of the chickens why the ribbons were there, he was told, "The ribbon protects them from the many vicious hawks that would otherwise attack them." The speaker went on to say, "I have been here fifteen years, and I have never known a hawk to take a chicken that had red ribbon on its back. The hawks seem to be afraid of that particular colour. Neither blue, nor green, nor any other colour seems to be effective in keeping away the robbers. I have seen hundreds of chickens taken when these hawks swoop down from the sky; but I have never seen a red-ribbon chicken go." Probably the patriarch Moses would have found interest in that story. It would have made him think of a night in Egypt when the scarlet stain on the door-posts warded off an attack of another kind. Life, the continuance of life, life everlasting, can only be guaranteed to those sheltered beneath the precious blood of Christ.

He Preferred to Hang

Dr. Robert G. Lee, the renowned preacher and author, has told a stirring story on pages 35 and 36 of his challenging book, *The Sinner's Saviour*. In his masterly way he indicates the value of accepting a pardon, and to do so draws from one of the strange incidents in American history. He says, "The difference between salvation provided in the death of

Christ and the acceptance of the provisions made, is set forth by George Wilson. In 1830, George Wilson was tried by a United States court in Philadelphia for robbery and murder, and sentenced to be hanged. Andrew Jackson, President of the United States, pardoned him. But Wilson refused the pardon, and insisted that it was not a pardon unless he accepted it. That was a point of law never before raised. The Attorney-General of the United States said the law was silent on the point. The President called upon the Supreme Court to decide the issue, as the Sheriff must know whether to hang Wilson or not. Chief Justice John Marshall, ablest of lawyers, gave the following decision: ' A pardon is a paper, the value of which depends upon its acceptance by the person implicated. It is hardly to be supposed that one under sentence of death would refuse to accept a pardon; but if it is refused, it is no pardon. George Wilson must hang.' And he was hanged.

"Who was responsible for his death? No one but Wilson himself. The law said he must die. The President stepped in between him and the law, but the man refused his pardon. Indirectly, the Supreme Court of the United States decided that the atonement of Christ, in making provision for the salvation of the whole world, is only beneficial to those who receive Him as their own personal Saviour. . . ."

Dr. Lee is a famous preacher, whose influence has reached every part of America; but it is problematical whether in all his preachings, in all his very acceptable writings, he ever said or wrote anything more important than this striking paragraph.

Life everlasting is not for a day—for a week, month, or year. Life everlasting goes on endlessly through the countless ages of eternity. To bring this priceless treasure within reach of sinful man, the Lord Jesus was crucified. Now it can be proclaimed throughout the world: "The gift of God is eternal life." To refuse it is to sign one's own death warrant.

THE DIVINE LAWYER . . . and the dramas in the court house

(GENESIS 6:3)

There are two Bible words which, pregnant with meaning, offer the most suggestive word-pictures. Dr. Strong declares that the Hebrew word *doon,* translated *to strive,* really means to struggle to resist a charge of murder. Liddle and Scott maintain that the Greek word *agonizomai,* which is also translated *to strive,* means precisely the same thing. Therefore in order to appreciate the full significance of these Scriptures, one must endeavour to see a law court where a desperate lawyer anxiously examines the records, sifts each piece of evidence, and does everything possible to gain a verdict on behalf of the accused.

The Case that was Lost

The court house was in the open air, and possibly near to the forests which lined the sides of a mountain. In the valley stood the skeleton of a huge ship; and not far away was the ancient saw-mill, alongside of which were piles of saw-dust. Nearby stood a strange old man, who always refused to work on the Sabbath. His name was Noah. His ship was truly fantastic, but his preaching was even more so. All the people knew him, and probably thought he was mad. When he insisted that God would pour judgment upon the nation, they laughed him to scorn. What right had Noah, or even God, to interfere in their pleasures? They loved to do that which Noah condemned; he should mind his own business! They failed to understand that they were figures in a court of law. The judge was God; the prosecuting counsel was Righteousness; the counsel for the defence was the Holy Spirit; the junior counsel was Noah; the accused was a guilty world. Possibly a rowdy meeting had just ended when God said, " My spirit shall not always *strive* with man." The word used was *doon.* It might be translated, " My spirit shall not always struggle desperately to save the lives of sinful people." *How righteous are the laws of God.* The Holy Spirit acted as counsel for the defence; yet when no righteous escape could be found, love yielded to law and the sentence was passed. *How wonderful is the love of God.* That He should even try to save such people reveals a compassion beyond degree. *How persistent is the Spirit of God.* He continued year after year, and only gave up the struggle when to continue was virtually impossible.

9

The Case that was Won

Once again the court house was in the open air, where beneath the star-lit heavens the Son of God lay prostrate. Describing the scene, Luke declared, " And being in an *agony* he prayed more earnestly: and his sweat was as it were great drops of blood falling down to the ground " (Luke 22:44). The word translated *agony* is the Greek equivalent of the Hebrew word *doon,* and again suggests the desperation to offset a capital charge. Man was in danger; the forces of righteousness were about to pass sentence; the time was very short, but Christ was making the supreme effort to discover a loophole whereby the guilty could be saved from death. This was the climax of an epic struggle which had continued throughout the Saviour's life. Continually the forces of evil had tried to defeat this great Lawyer; but when victory seemed within their grasp, He seized the sin of the accused, suffered in his stead, and satisfied every requirement of divine justice. The Saviour of men died in His own court-house, and the prisoner went out free.

The Case that is Still in Doubt

There was a day when the disciples asked the Lord, " Are there few that be saved? " and His reply presented them with another word-picture. They saw a city on a hill-top; the sun was setting, and the gates were about to be closed. Certain travellers who were late were struggling desperately to reach the gate before it closed for the night, and some were finding difficulty in climbing the hill. They were hurrying; they were breathless: but to enter in time was a matter of supreme importance. The disciples were still visualising the scene when the voice of Jesus said, "Strive (*agonize*) to enter in at the strait gate: for many, I say unto you, will seek to enter in, and shall not be able " (Luke 13:24). The same desperation exhibited in the effort of the Holy Spirit in Noah's day, and in Christ's sacrifice in the garden of Gethsemane, should be found in our untiring desire to get into the Kingdom of God. There is so much at stake; there is no time to lose. This case may be either won or lost, and we shall be the deciding factors. What shall it profit a man if he gain the whole world and lose his soul?

The Cross in the Clouds

" *Fasten your safety belts."* The friendly, warm glow in the indicator panel had issued the command, and within seconds the air hostess moved between the seats making sure that the Captain's order had been obeyed. Ahead, the sky was very dark; obviously the aeroplane was flying into trouble. I was far from happy. During a brief stay in the airport at Toronto, I had heard news of the devastating storm which had reached the Prairie provinces of Canada, and my fears of coming discomfort now appeared to be completely justified. I remembered the passengers who had staggered from the Winnipeg plane; I wondered if I would even live to stagger from this plane! The young hostess smiled and said, " It's going to be a bit bumpy." She was a model of discretion, and should have been rewarded for her tact. The brilliant sunshine of early morning had disappeared; we were enveloped in gloom. The plane began lurching as if it had suddenly become a cork adrift in a tempest. I gripped the sides of the seat and prayed.

After forty minutes the gloom began to disappear, and I saw *the pilot's cross*—the shadow of our aircraft on the clouds. Patiently, persistently, it followed us, silently announcing that the storm was over; the sun was shining again. And as I considered its message, I remembered another Cross which broadcast an identical message. Even eternal storms subside when souls begin to appreciate the superlative worth of the death of Christ. I had food for thought, and soon was permitted to undo the safety belt. We were flying beneath blue skies once more; we were safe. I wondered if others had ever found comfort in *the pilot's cross,* and later in the city of Regina was thrilled to read the testimony of a kindred soul.

In the *Reader's Digest* for September, 1958, Ardis Whitman's article had been condensed from the American magazine, *The Christian Herald.* The writer said: " In the lives of all of us there are blazing instants of reality, moments when we suddenly seem to understand ourselves and the world. Once a pilot told me of an experience when he was flying a plane crowded with passengers. A sudden storm had struck just as they passed the dangerous defiles of the Rocky Mountains, and for a few terrible minutes he had not been sure they'd make it. Then with one final flash of lightning, one last crash of thunder, the storm broke away and they emerged into a tremulous sunlight. And now keeping pace with them as they flew, was that lovely symbol, *the pilot's cross*—the shadow of the plane on the clouds. Flung round it was a halo of light, and beyond that, the victorious circle of a rainbow. ' For a single instant,' he said, ' I saw the beauty and perfection of the world, and felt as if I were one with it.' It is in moments like these that we truly live. . . ."

The Imprisoned Angel

Michaelangelo, the immortal painter and sculptor of Italy, succeeded in carving his name upon the face of his country. Today, all over the land, in churches and other great buildings, guides proudly indicate the works of art which are pre-served with loving care. During the early summer of 1957 I visited Italy and saw many of these invaluable treasures. I shall always remember *The Angel,* and how the guide said, " This was once a piece of discarded marble in a builder's yard. Sculptors rejected it because of its many flaws. Then one day, Michaelangelo walked down the street and saw the block of marble in a corner of the yard. He paused to make enquiries, and was told it was worthless. He replied, ' I see an angel in it.' " The famous sculptor began his task, and from that shapeless, unattractive piece of dirty marble pro-duced his angelic masterpiece.

I know Another whose rare vision enables Him to see worth in worthless things. I have watched as He carved angels out of flaw-filled humans. It is not too much to say that only His interest prevented our being rejected for ever.

Years ago, in the place which is now called Kimberley, in South Africa, children played with attractive pieces of " glass " which they had found on the veldt. A stranger passed, and looking closely at the glass recognised diamonds. He too went to work, and today the Kimberley mines are among the greatest in the world. Vast quantities of wealth have been taken from the earth, and these sparkling diamonds have found their way to all parts of the globe. Yet had not the stranger recognised the true worth of *the worthless glass,* scintillating gems would have remained buried in the dark-ness. In all these facts are living parables. Let us rejoice in the knowledge and love of the Saviour, and remember that without His aid, we too might have been left unwanted and alone.

A HAND, A DOOR, AND A KNOCK

(GENESIS 7:10; REVELATION 3:20; MATTHEW 25:10-11)

I have often been asked, "If God knew that man would sin, why did He create him?" The question, however, presents only a negative approach to a vital theme. We might also ask, "If God knew that millions of men would find and enjoy eternal happiness, would He have been justified in *not* creating man because some people would choose unwisely?" There are two sides to every picture; and whatever we may decide concerning this problem, one thing remains indisputable—man *was* created. Furthermore, he was given a free will. Varying circumstances may influence him; strong pressure may be brought to bear upon him; but always, man has the power to choose. When we unite three Scriptures, this fact is plainly visible.

The Hand that Never Knocked

Noah's strange craft loomed against the blue sky, and around it, sightseers asked innumerable questions. Surely this Master-carpenter was a fool! He had worked without wages for many years. He apparently served an employer who neither came to see the job, nor remembered to send payment to the man who did it. Yet Noah continued his labours. When he took time off, he devoted it to preaching; and his message was the most fantastic story the people had ever heard. Probably they listened to the strange old man and decided he was good fun! When he rebuked their sin, they tolerated him; when he spoke of the holiness of God, they probably frowned and denied their sinfulness; when he said the time of retribution was at hand, they undoubtedly laughed him to scorn. When Noah's predictions came true, they were dumbfounded and overwhelmed; yet seven days of priceless opportunity elapsed between Noah's entering the ark and the fulfilment of his prophecy. If, during that period, any man had knocked in faith on the door of the ark, he would have been admitted.

The Hand that Always Knocks

"Behold, I stand at the door, and knock: if any man will . . ." "If any man *will* . . ." Surely we may repeat an earlier statement—man has not changed. (i) *They were very satisfied.* They said, "We are rich, and increased with goods, and have need of nothing." Perhaps this was the secret of their folly. Few men can offset the challenge and temptation of prosperity. A nation is easier to reach in war than it is in peace-time; a man engulfed by poverty is more susceptible to the Gospel than a wealthy financier whose attitude proclaims to the world " he has need of nothing." (ii) *They were very surprised.* Surely it was inexcusable arrogance to say to such fine people, " Thou art wretched, and miserable, and poor, and blind, and naked." such statements were irresponsible: and thereby hangs profound truth. A man may measure himself against a mountain and feel a midget; the same man may measure himself against a mouse and feel a giant. Man's standards may pronounce him great; God's standards might reveal him to be small and useless. (iii) *They were very stupid.* The Lord Jesus was kept waiting at the door. Constantly He had knocked, seeking admission; but the " need of nothing" attitude had made the people complacently at ease. After all, they did not need Him; they were doing very well without Him. Poor Laodicea!

The Hand that Knocked Too Late

When asked for signs of His return, the Lord Jesus spoke of ten virgins who went forth to meet a bridegroom. He said, " And five of them were wise, and five were foolish." They all heard the same message; to a degree they all shared the same desire—to be present at the forthcoming celebrations. They were different only in that five were so anxious about their reception that they were careful to attend to every detail necessary to ensure their readiness. The other five were contentedly at ease. They were neither fussy nor fearful. They fully expected to be there, and without any fear lay down to sleep. Their attitude said, " Please do not disturb us. We are fully aware of everything; we have need of nothing; when the bridegroom comes, we shall be as ready and as well-equipped as all others." The people of Noah's day, the citizens of Laodicea, and the five foolish virgins, appear to be strangely related—related to our generation. " Afterward came also the other virgins, saying, Lord, Lord, open to us. But he answered and said, Verily, I say unto you, I know you not." They knocked on the door, but they knocked too late. Happy is that man who remembers: " Now is the accepted time; now is the day of salvation."

The Negro's Testimony

Dr. Harry A. Ironside will long be remembered. His forthright messages, his living illustrations, and the manner in which he put these to his ever-widening audiences, revealed him to be outstanding as a preacher. It was no cause for amazement when crowds flocked to hear him; and everywhere one heard appreciations of his dynamic ministry. Among the choicest of his stories was one concerning a

Negro who rose to give a testimony in a certain meeting. In his quaint but delightful manner the coloured Christian praised the Lord for the grace that had found and reclaimed him. His language was colourful, and the majority of his listeners enthusiastic. However, the chairman of that service was not evangelistic in his outlook, and his liberal view of spiritual matters included a strong emphasis on man's part in working out God's salvation. He listened to the Negro's testimony, and as this continued, became rather restless—it seemed too one-sided in its emphasis. When the opportunity came, the chairman rose to say, " Our brother has only spoken of one side of the great picture. He has told us something of what God did; he has forgotten to add *what he was required to do.* When I became a Christian, I had to clean up my house, and do many things before I could even expect God to do anything. Brother," he added, as he turned to face the Negro, " didn't you find that was the case with you? " Dr. Ironside in telling the story would smile as he imitated the Negro, who instantly replied, " Yes, Sah, Ah clean done forgot. Ah didn't tell you 'bout my part, did I? Well, Ah did my part for over thirty years, running away from God as fast as evah my feet could carry me. That was my part. An' God took aftah me till He run me down. That was His part."

And that about sums it up. From Eden until Olivet, from Pentecost until the present time, God has always done the seeking. Eternal love for sinners guarantees that sooner or later He will arrive to knock at the door of a man's life, and say, " Behold, I stand at the door, and knock. . . . If any man will open the door . . . I will come in. . . ."

The Meeting in Hell

My first pastor was the late Rev. Arthur Harries, whose ministry is still recalled in the mining valleys of Wales. He was an eloquent preacher of the Gospel, and probably did more to mould my young Christian life than any other. Some of his sermons, alas, were too deep for a boy's understanding; but as a man, he was superb. I have since discovered that one of his most effective illustrations came from *The Biblical Treasury.* Arthur Harries had an extensive library, and used it to good advantage.

A certain minister had been working hard preparing his sermon for the following Sunday, but in some strange way the essence of what he desired to say continued to elude him. His text was to be, " Now is the accepted time; behold, now is the day of salvation." Suddenly he fell asleep, to dream that he had somehow reached the abyss in eternity. A meeting of demons was in session, and the problem of how best to seduce men was being debated with enthusiasm. One demon volunteered to go to earth to deceive the mind of man. He said, " I will tell them that the Bible is all wrong; that its stories are legendary; that it does not mean what it says." This idea was discarded, for the majority considered man to be too intelligent to accept such heresy. Then another demon offered to come to earth to say, "There is no God, no Saviour, no heaven, no hell." But again the offer was rejected, as it seemed highly problematical whether the majority of earthlings would accept the denial. The entire meeting seemed bewildered until one demon, wiser than his fellows, rose to say, " No; I will journey to the world of men and tell them that *there is a God*. I will tell them that there is a Saviour, and a heaven and a hell. Yes, I will assure them that this is all true; but then I will whisper in their ears that there is no need to hurry. I will tell them there is plenty of time; that they may enjoy the pleasures of sin first, and at some time in the future begin thinking of eternal things." And all the demons in hell rose to acclaim his wisdom—and then they sent him to earth!

" Mr. Powell," said a lady to me in New Zealand, " please pray for my husband. Unless something happens to rouse him, he'll die. He sits week after week thinking, thinking. He never goes out; he hardly eats, and sleep seems impossible. He says God called him to be a missionary. He maintains that God called him to full-time service; that he refused, stayed at home, and married, and now it's too late to do much about it. Please pray for him." I did, but what more could I do? The man was correct. It *was* too late.

LOT'S WIFE . . . and a striking sequence of thought

When the disciples asked the Lord what would be the signs of His return, He replied, " Then shall two be in the field; the one shall be taken, and the other left. Two women shall be grinding at the mill; the one shall be taken, and the other left. Watch therefore: for ye know not what hour your Lord doth come " (Matt. 24:40-42). Mankind divides into two classes, and this fact is revealed throughout the Bible.

Lot Who Lost His Wife—Genesis 19:23-26

Lot was thunderstruck! He could hardly believe his eyes. Even now he wondered if he were dreaming. "Escape for thy life " still rang in his ears, and he was left in no doubt that God had sent two angels to warn him about the catastrophe soon to overwhelm Sodom. Hurriedly he had done his best to persuade the members of his family, but his sons-in-law had laughed him to scorn; they probably said his story was fantastic. His wife and daughters, however, had listened to his words, and now they were to hurry to safety. Alas, Lot was destined to lose his wife. She was a runaway who forgot to take her heart. "But his wife looked back from behind him, and she became a pillar of salt." She heard the same message, she had access to the same facts, but she perished within sight of her husband's refuge.

Abigail Who Lost Her Husband—1 Samuel 25

They were a strange couple, as unlike as it was possible to be, and quite unsuited to each other. " Abigail was a woman of good understanding, and of a beautiful countenance: but her husband was churlish and evil in all his doings. . . ." (v.3). They were wealthy and well protected; they had been most fortunate, for during perilous days David and his men had safeguarded their flocks and herds. Alas, the wealthy farmer had more money than sense! When David's followers asked for succour—a due reward for help given—they were insulted and driven away. " And behold, Nabal held a feast in his house, like the feast of a king; and his heart was merry within him, for he was drunken" (v. 36). Within a few hours the hand of judgment approached the household, and in the events which followed, the one was taken and the other left.

The Thief Who Lost His Comrade—Luke 23:39-43.

Did they know each other well? They had been comrades in life; they were now to die together. Matthew reminds us that they went to their crosses using identical language. "The thieves, also, which were crucified with him, cast the same in his teeth" (Matt. 27:44). These unfortunate men were both near the Lord; they heard the same words from His lips, and yet their reactions to His message were strangely different. In response to the faith of the penitent thief, Christ said, "Today shalt thou be with me in paradise." Alas, only one was taken; the other was left. Sunshine melts wax but hardens clay; and it would seem that God's love acts similarly on human hearts. Some yield—others resist—it depends upon the nature of the individual heart.

The Mill Girl Who Lost Her Workmate—Matthew 24:41

The workroom was a scene of activity; the girls were busy at their machines. Tons of grain were being fed methodically into the waiting rollers; at the end of the line, the gaping mouths of empty sacks waited for the crushings which ran as water from the shining steel trays. How different this modern mill from the ancient ones where two women laboriously pushed around the long handle which in turn operated the stone which ground the corn. Two women worked on. One was thoughtful, the other carefree and gay. One was religious; she expected the coming of her Lord. The other was worldly and indifferent to the claims of Christ. The one prayed, the other sneered. Then quite suddenly it happened. "The one was taken, the other left." Consternation spread over the face of the second woman; she was surprised and frightened. Where was her workmate? She had been there a moment before; what had happened to take her away so quickly? And then a shout came from other parts of the mill. Many more people had vanished. It was all a nightmare; the machinery was switched off, questions were asked; but the Lord had come, and "one had been taken and the other left." In this way, and in so many words, Jesus described events to precede His return into this world. Through the medium of the Church, the second advent message is being proclaimed far and wide. Signs among the nations, the fulfilment of prophecy, and the urgent need of our tottering world, suggest that the coming of Christ will soon take place. If he should come today, would we be taken, or left? Would we be ready to welcome Him, or left to remember our stupidity?

The Two Boys in Blantyre

David Livingstone has always been my hero-missionary, and that probably accounts for the fact that I have seized every opportunity to visit the places with which he was associated. Toward the close of my four years' itinerary in

Southern Africa, I stood in the most sacred of all African places—the clearing in the forest where the indomitable missionary knelt to pray his way into the eternal kingdom. I remembered the devotion of the carrier boys who later took the body of their friend six hundred miles to the coast, so that it might be taken to his own country. My friends and I spoke of these memorable events, and then had a prayer meeting in which we asked God to kindle such fires of devotion and enthusiasm in our own hearts. Finally we spoke of the incident which has now been told around the world. As the missionary's funeral passed along the crowded streets of London, one old man wept bitterly. Later, this poor fellow explained how he had been the boyhood friend of Livingstone. They had lived and played together in Blantyre, Scotland. When Livingstone surrendered himself to Christ, the boys drifted apart, for his friend remained unsaved. The old man added, " Now Davy is honoured by everybody, but I am a poor old drunkard."

" No One Ever Asked ME "

Dr. Jerome O. Williams, one of the Southern Baptist leaders in America, has written a delightful book called, *Let Me Illustrate*. It is easy to read, inspiring, and exceedingly helpful for young ministers. Dr. Williams tells the story of a Negro boy of about twelve years of age. At first, the lad was unwilling to accept a ride in the minister's carriage, for he said his shoes were muddy, and his getting into the clean buggy would spoil it. However, the kindly pastor persuaded the lad to get in; and as they rode along together, they conversed about the community—the schools, and eventually the church. Dr. Williams then said, " Jim, do you know anything about Jesus? " Immediately the lad's face was aglow, and his eyes sparkled as he said, " He's de Saviour." Dr. Williams continues: " After asking him if he thought the Lord would save the people of Europe, Asia, and the other continents, and getting a positive answer, I said, ' Jim, do you believe Jesus will save the coloured people? ' He replied, ' I tells ye, Boss,. He's everybody's Saviour? ' I looked into his face and said, ' Jim, is He your Saviour? ' With this question his head dropped, his eyes flashed far more slowly as great tears began to trickle down his black cheeks. When he seemed to be ready for further conversation, I said, ' Well, Jim, you must have found something wrong with Him if you cannot accept Him as your personal Saviour.' He was immediate and positive in his reply that there was nothing wrong at all with Jesus as the Saviour, and said again, ' He's everybody's Saviour.' ' Well, then,' I enquired, ' Why have you never taken Him as your own

Saviour? ' He was very pathetic as he looked into my face, and with a most pitiful appeal in his eyes said, 'No one has ever asked me to take Him.'"

Dr. Williams explained how the lad could become a Christian, and soon the boy was saying—and again I quote, "'I can accept Him; I will accept Him; I do accept Him. He's my Saviour. I take Him as mine . . .' When he began to rejoice, he forgot his muddy feet, his wet clothes, and the filled bucket, and spilled buttermilk all over the buggy. . . . As we drove along . . . he came to himself, looked about, and said, 'Law, white man, I oughtta got out o' dis buggy two miles back over yonder! ' "

No one had ever asked him to be a Christian. That seems to have been the one supreme mistake made by each of the wise virgins. Instead of seeking to win a sister, the five wise virgins went to sleep. Consequently, when the Bridegroom came, they were taken, but *the others were left.*

" Sir, I was the one left "

He was a fine young man of about 20 years, but his face suggested he had known difficult days. His sister sat alongside, and her eyes were moist. She had prayed for her brother, and now, at the conclusion of a Gospel meeting in Montreal, Canada, her prayers were to be answered. "Sir," he said, "I have just come from Hungary. I was a student when the Communists butchered our people. Actually, I had taken no part in the fighting, but the soldiers made me help carry a stretcher to remove dead bodies from the streets of our city. It was awful, for the night was filled with the sounds of exploding bombs. Then the stretcher dropped, and when I turned to look, my pal who was helping to carry the dead, had himself been killed. His face had been shot away. I felt very sick, but they made me carry on. Yes, I was the one left. I think I know the reason. My sister was praying for me. Oh, sir, I want to be a Christian. Perhaps that is why God spared me."

ANAH . . . who chased donkeys

(GENESIS 36:24)

Anah was a stay-at-home boy who resisted the desire to go forth in search of independence and fame. His name should be printed in letters of gold. Names can be most uninteresting, and the long lists in this chapter of Genesis frighten the casual reader. ". . . Lotan, and Shobal, and Zibeon, and Anah, and Dishon, and Ezer, and Dishan: these are the dukes of the Horites, the children of Seir in the land of Edom. And the children of Lotan were Hori and Hemam, and . . ." If names were sandhills, Genesis 36 would be a desert. Names, names, lots of names; a desert indeed: but in the midst of barrenness stands an oasis. ". . . this was that Anah that found the mules in the wilderness, as he fed the asses of Zibeon his father." The Revised Version sheds increased light upon the text, for the word translated "mules" should be *hot springs*.

Some Great Decisions

Anah lived in days when a far-reaching world offered amazing opportunities. Beyond the horizons were unclaimed expanses of virgin soil, where cattle increased and men became dukes in their own right. Sites for cities were offered free of charge; and the challenge of the unknown was almost irresistible. Fathers were never surprised when their sons went forth to stake claims to greatness. The number of dukes increased a hundredfold, and the little stay-at-home boy seemed either a coward or a fool. Undoubtedly he knew all about the mighty exploits of his valiant brethren, and he too would have loved to be the head of a great people. Yet he bowed at another altar—the altar of duty; and when he arose, went in search of his father's asses. Instead of erecting a great city, he reared stubborn donkeys; instead of making money, he spread out fodder. A commendable young fool!

Some Glamourless Duties

One day he had to seek further than was usual; the stupid donkeys had wandered. He followed their trail through the bush into strange territory. He called, but they would not respond. He continued to search; and when he saw the animals peacefully grazing beside bubbling springs in the wilderness, poor Anah probably wondered if he were suffering from sunstroke. Springs in the wilderness; an oasis in the desert—impossible! He rubbed his eyes; but when he looked again the scene was unaltered. It was unbelievable. Anah was thrilled by a new excitement. This was no mirage, but a glorious reality; he had found hot springs in the wilderness. This discovery would revolutionise his family's future. He would be famous, wealthy, envied. Surely he felt like kissing his donkeys—the stubborn little darlings. They were the loveliest of all animals; they were angels in disguise. They had led him to a gold-mine. How providential that he had preferred their company to that of the mighty dukes of the Horites!

Some Glorious Discoveries

Anah's wilderness is all around us; his asses are wonderfully familiar. (i) *Teaching naughty boys in a difficult Sunday-school class.* The modern Anah sometimes has to choose between the weekly duty and a wonderful picnic on the warm, inviting sands at the seashore. The glamour of the one is as great as the boredom of the other. Boys—rude, unappreciative young hooligans—my Father's asses! If one of them became a medical missionary, I too would have found hot springs in a wilderness. (ii) *Nursing grumbling patients in a hospital ward.* My Father's asses resemble the people who constantly cry, " Nurse, Nurse, Nurse! " Hard work and continuous attention are rewarded by increasing complaint's which fray one's temper and irritate one's soul. Why should I stay when I could double my wages elsewhere? Some nurses do it for Christ's sake, and thereby discover hot springs of healing for their deepest need. (iii) *Cooking for irritable people in a selfish household.* Perhaps the most difficult of all tasks is that of the mother whose value is seldom realised until her hands cease to minister. One meal ends as another approaches; one complaint has hardly died before another is born. Cooking, darning, cleaning, washing, loving, enduring; and sometimes it seems so fruitless. Some mothers, some wives, have given up the struggle, and homes have crashed; others have lingered, to find hot springs in a wilderness—a boy has been won for Christ and sent into the ministry. (iv) *Preaching to critics in a dead church.* This is a desert indeed. These donkeys are unique! Poor Anah! Another church—or even a secular job, and he would become a duke! Sunday is coming, and he will be required to feed his Father's asses; and some will not even be there to be fed! Should he give up? No. There are Spurgeons and Wesleys still to be won. Even the wilderness may blossom as the rose if I know how to do things " for my Father's sake."

The Saviour's Apple Tree

One of the most entrancing booklets I have ever seen is entitled *Our Daily Bread*. It is published by the co-editors, M. R. De Haan and H. G. Bosch, in connection with the

Radio Bible Class, at Grand Rapids, Michigan. These servants of God have a gift for gathering together the most charming illustrations, and their publication must bring immeasurable happiness to all their readers. In the September, 1958, edition, H. G. Bosch re-tells three short but vital stories, which illustrate the basic facts of the account where Anah chased his donkeys.

"Mother," said a sweet Christian girl one evening, "I want you to give me a little apple tree in our orchard." "Why, my child, they are all yours, for they belong to our family." "Yes, but I mean something different. I should like to have a little tree for my very own; and the apples which it bears, I would like to give as a present to the Lord." The child was allowed to choose a tree. Laying her hand on the trunk, she said, "Little tree, now you belong to the Lord Jesus." Some time later the mother sent a gift to some missionaries, and after relating the above incident, continued, "Our little one was suddenly taken home to be with the Lord. She has now been a year in heaven, and this year the tree bore fruit for the first time. I am enclosing what we received from the sale of the apples." This little child was no great preacher going forth to move and conquer cities; she stayed in her orchard, from which her actions sent fragrance around the world.

Ministering Hands

The Rev. Ira Gillett, missionary to Portuguese East Africa, tells of a group of natives who made a long journey, walking past a nearby Government hospital, to come to his mission station for treatment. When asked why they had travelled the extra miles to reach the mission hospital, when the same medicines were available at the Government institution, they replied, "The medicines may be the same, *but the hands are different.*" This statement is most illuminating; it reflects the quality of the service rendered by God's servants on the mission field. The love of God had been shed abroad in their hearts, and patients from near and far were quick to recognise the fact. Perhaps some of those missionaries felt their work was difficult and mediocre. There was neither glamour nor the financial gains offered in other spheres of labour; yet these wonderful people continued to work faithfully for the Master, and as a result found "hot springs in the wilderness."

Ruining the Clock

There was once an old "Grandfather" clock that had stood for three generations in the same corner, faithfully ticking off the minutes, hours, and days. In it was a heavy weight, which was pulled to the top each night in order to keep the clock running. "Too bad," thought the new owner, "that such an old clock should have to bear so great a load." So he took the heavy weight off the hook, and removed it from the clock. At once the old clock stopped ticking. "Why did you do that?" asked the clock. "I wanted to lighten your load," answered the man. "Please," said the clock, "put it back. That is what keeps me going." British readers will undoubtedly recall the famous radio show in which Mrs. Mopp, after regularly announcing her grumbles and complaints, came to a triumphant conclusion by saying, with a queer little laugh, "It's being so cheerful that keeps me going." Mrs. Mopp was very near to reality, for oftentimes the things which promote complaints keep us near to God. The path of life may abound with obstacles; the usual day-to-day routine of life may be monotonous and dreary; yet when these things are endured and conquered for the Lord's sake, any man is capable of finding hot springs in a desert.

God Sent Her to Hospital

Years ago a charming young Christian woman contracted tuberculosis, and was sent to the Sully Hospital, in South Wales. At first she was heart-broken, and her faith was sorely tested. I was asked to visit her, and with God's help, tried to reassure her that "all things work together for good to those who love the Lord." She smiled and tried to believe the text. Within weeks, her requests to the authorities, and my willingness to help, gained permission for Sunday services to be held in that magnificent hospital. Soon I was leading patients to Christ, and a welcome awaited me whenever I found time to visit the wards. When the widening circles of my ministry took me out of Great Britain, others stepped in to continue the work, and for sixteen years the Gospel has been preached regularly in that institution. The Christian girl soon returned to her home completely cured; but before she went, she found hot springs in the wilderness.

RADIANT FACES . . . reflecting the glory of God

(EXODUS 34:29-30; MATTHEW 17:1, 2; ACTS 6:15)

It has often been said that a man's face is a mirror reflecting his soul. As a general rule this must be true, for when a man is disturbed, he frowns; when he is pleased, his countenance reveals satisfaction; when he is overcome by grief, his face inevitably reveals anguish. This is also true in the realm of the spirit. If a man loves sin, his face betrays the habits of evil living. If a man serenely looks into the face of his Lord, the glory of the Infinite leaves a glow upon his countenance. There is a sun-tan which is the hall-mark of heaven! "They looked unto Him and were radiant."

The Resplendent Moses

"And it came to pass, when Moses came down from Mount Sinai . . . that Moses wist not that the skin of his face shone while he talked with God." Surely the secret of this facial illumination lay in the fact that Moses had talked *with* God. Much of what we call prayer-time is only a waste of time. We leave our prayers until we are either too tired or too busy to pray, and consequently our intercession is but a succession of requests made prior to some hurried departure either for the office or for slumberland. Prayer is a telephone talk with God. The man who truly prays, not only talks—*he listens*. It is most beneficial to share our problems with God, and to ask for divine assistance; but *the man who fails to listen never discovers the true power of prayer*. Prayer performs miracles; but not the least of these is that which changes the man himself. Moses lingered long enough to tell his troubles to God, and also to receive instructions relating to future conduct. Experimentally, he had known fellowship with his Maker; a radiant glow had been left on his face. Listening to God was just as important as speaking to God.

The Redeeming Master

"And after six days, Jesus taketh Peter, James, and John his brother . . . up into an high mountain apart, and was transfigured before them: and his face did shine as the sun. . . ." It is certainly thought-provoking that this was the only time when the phenomenon occurred. At no other time was it said, "His face did shine as the sun, and his raiment was white as the light." Surely some strange and wonderful

25

thing was taking place. Temporarily the Lord had left the valley of need, and had climbed into the stillness of the mountain to enjoy fellowship with His Father. It was this which ministered to the indefinable needs of His inmost being; and as His cup of spiritual satisfaction filled to the brim, His joy overflowed. Soon, as did Moses centuries earlier, the Lord would be required to return to the crowds; soon He would be confronted by increasing temptation. It was His holy fellowship in the mount which prepared Him for the eventualities of the future. He had talked with God, and that was the secret of His strength—it could be mine, too!

The Radiant Martyr

Stephen was in great danger; his accusers were determined to slay him. False witnesses were ready to make outrageous charges, and the stone-throwers were anxious to proceed with their foul plans. The brave Christian was not unaware of their desires as he stood before the Sanhedrin. He was calm, unruffled, dignified: "And all that sat in the council, looking steadfastly on him, saw his face as it had been the face of an angel." Their eyes condemned their actions, for soon "they stoned Stephen, calling upon God, and saying, Lord Jesus, receive my spirit. And he kneeled down, and cried with a loud voice, Lord, lay not this sin to their charge. And when he had said this, he fell asleep." Amidst such vile treachery, it was miraculous that Stephen's face should suggest angelic beauty. Surely it would have been easier to understand had his countenance revealed frustration, fear, or even angry defiance. When love, grace, and forgiveness emanated from the martyr's soul, the onlookers were supplied with first-class evidence that Stephen was no ordinary man. It was said that he was full of the Holy Spirit—he had mastered the art of *living with God,* and the resultant communion completely transformed his countenance. His face shone. True loveliness is something of the soul. It is character glorified, actions sanctified; the constant fulfilment in human life of the purposes of God. This holy sun-tan is the result of constant gazing into the face of the Sun of Righteousness.

Her Face Shone

My Sunday morning services were always broadcast throughout the hospital, and each one terminated with an announcement. "Listeners, I must leave now, in order to return to my own church service. But before I go, may I make a suggestion? If any listeners have a problem or a question; if you desire to see me personally, please tell Sister, and she will tell Matron. When I receive your message, I will come to see you."

It was visiting day, and as I walked through the main entrance of Sully Hospital, near Penarth, South Wales, Matron came forward to meet me. " Mr. Powell, —— wants to see you urgently. Would you please go and see what she wants? " I walked down the long corridor, and eventually reached her door. When I entered, my clerical collar immediately indicated that I was the minister. She had reddish hair, which perfectly matched her flushed complexion. Her eyes were spear-points of light; grim determination was stamped all over her face. Before I could say a word she said, "How are you, Father Powell? " I placed a chair near the foot of her bed, and calmly answered, "Just a minute; let's get one thing straight. I am *not* Father Powell! I am just a plain Baptist minister, and possibly I shall never be a father in my life! " She smiled and said, "Oh, that's all right with me, Father. I wanted to see you." I sighed and repeated my former statement; but I only wasted my breath, for she again said, "Don't worry, Father Powell, I wanted to see you urgently ". I remained Father Powell until the day of her death.

She told me how she had " had a row " with Father ——, and her chin seemed very pugnacious as she listed her grievances. She was a devout Roman Catholic, but in no uncertain fashion, so she informed me, she had told Father —— he could keep his religion : she would change to Father Powell's. When I interrupted to confess that my religion was no good, she was utterly amazed, and listened as I tried to explain that religion was never very much good. What man needed was not a dead religion, but a real faith in the Lord Jesus; to know Him as a living Friend. She was so puzzled; I might have been talking Dutch. It took a long time to make her understand, but finally I led her to Christ. Now she ranks as one of the most outstanding converts I ever met. She had been one of the greatest sinners, but the wonder of forgiveness filled her soul with peace.

" Mr. Powell, you are wanted urgently. That woman is dying. She is asking for you continually." I hurried to the hospital, and one look was sufficient to tell me my little friend was nearing home. I sat by her side and gently took her hand into mine; and I shall never forget what followed. For fully two minutes she gazed silently into my face, and then as a great sigh escaped her she said, " I wanted to see you once more; now—go away." I answered, "No, I intend to stay with you for a little while." She interrupted to say with emphasis, "No. Please go away." My face betrayed disappointment, and her eyes were quick to see the shadows.

" Ah, Mr. Powell, do not misunderstand me. I love you. I haven't any relatives. I haven't any friends. I haven't anybody in all this world except you. You introduced me to my Saviour, and I shall always love you. But, Mr. Powell, He has come to fetch me—He is here *now*. Oh, sir, as long as you sit there, I want to look at you; I want to speak to you. But there is Another present, and I want you to go away so that I can look at Him, and talk to Him all the time. But, sir, I wanted to see you once more before He takes me home." She stopped; her effort had drained her strength. My voice was very shaky when I whispered, " I understand. I'll see you *in the morning*." Reaching the door I turned to see her for the last time, but already she had forgotten me. She was looking straight ahead, and " the skin of her face shone." For a moment I was startled—I really was. Then I closed the door, and tip-toed down the corridor. Within a few hours I again passed her doorway, on my way to conduct the normal hospital service. I looked into the small room—and the bed was empty. I was left with my memories. As an ordinary window reflects the beauty of the setting sun until the glass seems to be made of gold, so her frail body reflected the indescribable glory of her Risen Lord.

THE PRIESTS . . . who were told to stay on a strict diet

(LEVITICUS 11 : 29-31)

Leviticus is the Book of the Priests; its teaching is devoted to the laws regulating the conduct of those who served in the temple. If we remember that a standard of holiness was required of all who ministered within the sanctuary, we shall easily understand the importance of the commands contained in this strange book. If we consider these things, we may find glimmerings of truth relating to a later generation of priests —those who through faith in the Saviour have been made kings and priests unto God. " These also shall be unclean unto you among the creeping things that creep upon the earth. . . ."

The Weasel

This little animal has never been popular. It is one of the most merciless and vicious trackers in the bush, and belies the beauty of its furry coat. When this creature gets on the trail of an innocent victim, it follows to the end. When the hunted one is cornered and cries out in fear, the weasel gloats over the prey and moves in for the kill. There are people of this type. They do not know the meaning of mercy.

The Mouse

There is not a great deal which may be said of the mouse, except that it lives in the dark, often gets into a hole, and is easily poisoned! It is more a nuisance than a danger, and seems to be gifted at upsetting old ladies! Its gnawing behind the scenes, and its habit of putting teeth into another's property, make it an outlaw.

The Tortoise

This creature lives in a house of armour. Ordinary weapons would only bounce from its back. They wander all over the place, and seem to have no settled home. Every night in certain countries motorists run over them, and yet seldom is one really hurt. They are errant knights in armour, and are very hard to reach. The tortoise is very slow, and has a habit of sticking its neck out!

The Ferret

This is the nastiest member of the family. It resembles a rat, and needs to be handled carefully. Its teeth are very sharp, and are capable of biting friend or foe. The ferret is never really happy unless it is hunting others; in this respect, it is closely related to the weasel. In the box or in the field, at work or in leisure moments, the ferret snaps, cannot be trusted, and its odour is never pleasant. The animal is prone to run wild, and may easily be lost forever.

The Chameleon

This is the most changeable creature in the world. It is difficult to see the animal, for its camouflage is perfect. On a green leaf, the chameleon turns green; on red leaves, it turns red. The chameleon likes to be in harmony with its environment. It has no abiding principles, except to be changeable as often as is necessary. Alas, this feature is one of the best-known characteristics of all people who have no convictions.

The Lizard

This is one of the smallest animals, but its tongue is deadly! This is most dangerous, and is often forked. When the lizard strikes, it does so with venom and accuracy. It has neither strong body nor powerful limbs; it is very timid, and runs away at the first sound of danger. Its tongue, however, is a rapier! It is doubtful whether this is ever used except to hurt, to capture, to destroy. Against such tendencies in human beings, Paul uttered his strongest warnings.

The Snail

This is a slimy creature! There are many parts of the world where snail shells are extremely beautiful; but all snails are slimy! They have never been known to do a good turn, they damage everything they touch, and can always be traced by their trails. Even if they possess an ornate palace in which to live, " they are wolves in sheep's clothing." Some people eat them; but there is no accounting for a man's taste!

The Mole

This small creature loves to burrow in the earth, and is always dirty. It hates the light, and lives in tiny tunnels in the ground. Farmers hate it; hunters trap it; none like it. A most unpopular and unfriendly creature, famous for spoiling fields.

The ancient priests were required to be fastidious; their's was a strict diet. There is a sense in which all Christians should emulate their example!

The Dead Seagulls

During my stay in Western Canada, I knew the pleasure of working with the Rev. Elgar Roberts, the Baptist Radio Padre; and from him I heard the following story. We were discussing the disappointing state of certain churches, when Mr. Roberts casually recalled a story he had heard a Welsh minister telling some years earlier. His friend had recently returned from a tour of Great Britain, and was describing how he had watched certain villagers removing dead seagulls from a sandy beach. The unfortunate birds had in some way been killed, and their bodies were scattered all over the sea shore. The visitor asked one of the workmen why the birds had died, and the following explanation was given.

" Sir, during the season, we get thousands of tourists here, and they feed our birds with sweets and candy, and other things harmful to sea birds. These gulls did not have the sense to know what was good for them. Month after month they fed on this unnatural food, and as a result lost their taste for their natural food. Then when the tourists went away, our seagulls had nothing to eat, and died of starvation. It was a pity, sir, but we couldn't do anything about it."

A similar tragedy has overtaken certain sections of the church. People have been fed so long with the pleasurable items of worldly food, that they have now lost their spiritual appetite. Then in times of stress and strain, when worldliness is unobtainable, the church members seem to weaken and die. Probably the best way to decide the ideal diet for the church is to discover what she ate during the days of her triumphs. There have been times when the challenge and power of the church enthralled a world; when every service was crowded; when thousands of people hurried to hear her preachers. The following details stand out as beacons on a dark night. The authority and love for the Word of God; the popularity of the prayer meetings as a means of grace; the desire for personal consecration; the increasing urge to win souls for Christ. When these things were in a place of priority, the wings of the assembly were sufficiently strong to carry the church into the very presence of God. Alas, the authority of the Bible has been questioned by leaders who suggested that the ancient records were only legends. Prayer meetings have been removed in favour of church dances. Personal consecration is often considered a fanatical unnecessary. Sundays present a great opportunity to play golf with business associates—if we are to win our friends, we must be like them! It is true to state that many people have lost their taste for spiritual things, and are dying.

The Sleeping Monkey

Petticoat-lane is one of London's street markets, and every Sunday morning, visitors see sights which beggar description. It has been said that a man may steal your watch at one end of the lane, and offer to sell it back to you at the other end. The most fabulous bargains are offered to gullible customers at ridiculous prices, and most visitors come away wondering how and why they were persuaded to spend their money. I shall always remember my first visit to Petticoat-lane. I had an hour to spare before my departure for Italy, and knowing I was close to this world-famous centre, I decided to go and see what I had often imagined. The crowds, the stalls, the bargains, were all as I expected; but one small animal seemed more attractive than all else.

An ex-service man was slowly moving along the street playing his barrel organ, but there was nothing very musical about the tunes which came from the old instrument. Round and round went the handle, and out came the saddening music. Yet the man never lacked an audience, for he possessed the cutest little monkey I had ever seen. The tiny animal held a bag, and each time a coin was offered, the proud young monkey looked at it, and then gave an immaculate salute to the donor. I watched for a considerable time, and felt my visit was worth while if only to see this delightful act. When opportunity occurred I spoke to the organ man, and was somewhat amused by his complaint. " Yes, sir, the other day a barrow boy came along and offered Joe a sweet. My monkey loves sweets, and as you can see, readily takes them from his admirers. That barrow boy gave him a sleeping pill, and Joe slept from Sunday morning until Thursday. Aye, sir, it was a dirty trick."

I have often thought about that monkey, and have wondered how often a similar occurrence has happened to Christians. The evil one seems to have mastered the art of putting sleeping pills into the tasty sweet-meats upon which we like to indulge. Perhaps if we were as fastidious as were the ancient priests, our spiritual health would improve tremendously.

THE ARCHANGEL ... who started the ball rolling

(DEUTERONOMY 34:5-6; JUDE 9)

The hillside was still; even the birds hushed their chatter. The grand old man of Israel stood gazing toward the land of which he had thought constantly for nearly forty years. Ahead lay the land of Canaan; behind, in the plains, were his beloved people—he would see them no more. His life was almost over; he had come to the mountain to attend his own funeral! The angels were preparing the grave when Moses turned and fell into the everlasting arms. "And God buried him in a valley in the land of Moab: but no man knoweth of his sepulchre unto this day."

The Angel Who Protected the Worship—Jude 9

The men were climbing the mountain. Their eyes were red with weeping, but a steady unflinching purpose filled their souls. Their beloved Moses was dead, but only now had they come to appreciate his true greatness. They were determined to rectify matters. His body should be honoured, and if necessary retained so that future generations could pay homage to the revered patriarch. Somewhere in the upper valleys of the lofty hills, they would find his grave; they would search until they succeeded. And just beyond the bounds of the visible, Satan smiled. He would stand, so to speak, over the secret grave and beckon the seekers. He would guide them; he would lead them to the spot. "Yet Michael the archangel, when contending with the devil, *disputed about the body of Moses* . . . and said, The Lord rebuke thee" (Jude 9). Again and again the searching men walked past the grave, but the green turf gave no indication that it had become a shroud. Thus did God prevent Israel from committing a great sin. There is every reason to believe that had they found the body of Moses, they would have worshipped the casket. The archangel's intervention prevented the people from stumbling, and at the same time started a ball rolling through the centuries.

The Answer which Protected the Witness—Matthew 17:24-27

Simon Peter was pre-occupied; his face betrayed the disturbance in his soul. Something was wrong! "And when they were come to Capernaum, they that received tribute money came to Peter, and said, Doth not your Master pay tribute?

He said, Yes. And when he was come into the house, Jesus prevented him saying, What thinkest thou, Simon? . . ." And that simple question uncovered the doubts in Peter's mind. Had they paid their taxes? He had no knowledge of any such payment. Would the officials be a nuisance and prosecute the Lord?—and Peter's face darkened. After a little instruction, Christ said to His servant, " Notwithstanding, *lest we should offend them,* go thou to the sea, and take up the fish that first cometh up; and when thou hast opened his mouth, thou shalt find a piece of money: that take, and give unto them for me and thee." The Lord's precautionary measures prevented people from stumbling. His was a great example.

The Apostle Who Protected the Work—Romans 14: 13-23

Christianity was not the continuation of Judaism, for in the fellowship of the new movement Christians enjoyed liberty unknown under law. Under the old régime it was an offence to eat certain meat; under grace, it was not. On the other hand, idolators practised rites which demanded certain offerings, and the meat associated with these was an integral part of something condemned by Christian teachers. It was no cause for amazement, therefore, when men began arguing as to whether certain meat should, or should not, be eaten. Finally Paul wrote his classic message dealing with this subject. " Let us not therefore judge one another any more . . . let no man put a stumbling block or an occasion to fall in his brother's way . . . But if thy brother be grieved with thy meat, now walkest thou not charitably. Destroy not him with thy meat, for whom Christ died . . . It is good neither to eat flesh, nor to drink wine, nor anything whereby thy brother stumbleth, or is offended, or is made weak . . . " Certain things may be quite harmless, but a Christian manifests greatness in abstaining from such " *for his brother's sake.*" We are living epistles, seen and read of all men. To abstain for my brother's sake is to walk a royal highway.

In conclusion, it might be beneficial to study a contrast. The New Testament church had at least one member whose carnal attitude kept many from the Lord's table. John wrote of him, " Diotrephes, who loveth to have the pre-eminence among them, received us not . . . prating against us with malicious words: and not content therewith, neither doth he himself receive the brethren, he forbiddeth them that would, and casteth them out of the church " (3 John 9, 10). It is a sad event when the Sun of Righteousness is eclipsed by stupid people. The fact that my example may help or hinder a fellow man should stimulate me to walk circumspectly all the days of my life.

During the summer of 1927, I visited the Overcomer Testimony Convention at Swanwick, Derbyshire, England, and met the quiet clergyman whose story I am about to tell. He was sad, and thoughtful. When a question was asked concerning the advisability of frequenting places of worldly amusement, he inclined his head. Others were eloquent in announcing their opinions, but the dignified minister held his peace. Later, my own pastor explained the man's reluctance to talk, and as I heard the following story, my soul was stirred.

That minister had been asked to visit a very sick lady; and when he entered the bedroom, he saw instantly that she was dying. Her face revealed signs of an unfortunate past; he realised he was in the presence of a great sinner. When he spoke, her attitude seemed rather cynical. Her smiles were mirthless; her scornful eyes were not in harmony with her face. The minister became nonplussed, and had difficulty in continuing the conversation. Then she asked her first question.

" Do you know that I am dying?"

" Well, you are very ill, but——"

" I'm dying, and we both know it. But do you know why I am dying? Do you know what is the matter with me? Perhaps I had better tell you. I am dying because of my sin. My disease is not nice to mention—you understand. Do you know how all this came about?"

The clergyman was bewildered. Perhaps coming events were casting their shadows before—and the first shadows were already falling across his soul. With deadly purpose, she repeated her question. " Do you know how all this came about? I'll tell you. *You led me astray.* No, don't interrupt until I have told you everything. At one time you were a commercial traveller. I knew you even in those days. You were a leader in your church, but your duties took you away from home during the week. Do you remember being in a certain town—I was there, too. I saw you one night going into a certain place. I suppose you were a bit lonely; you had nowhere to go. It was a cold, damp night, and you seemed a bit fed up. Do you remember? I was surprised, for you were a leader of the church at home. I was cold and fed up, too, but I hadn't quite as much money as you had. I stood in the street and considered that if you could do that kind of thing, it would be safe to follow your example. So I followed you; but that night I met certain undesirable people, and before we were through, my soul had been damned. That was only the beginning. Many things have happened since then, and now I'm finished. My body is finished, and my soul is finished. You led me astray. If I had not followed your example, I might have remained a good woman. That's all; I wanted you to know what you did for me."

When I met him, that minister was very quiet. He never argued; he was trying to forget the unforgettable.

The President's Choice

" Little things can reveal a person's character. Our words can impress others, and make them think we are dedicated to a great task. But a small act, which we think goes unnoticed, may tear down all we claim to be. President William McKinley once had to decide between two men, equally qualified, for appointment as foreign minister. He told later how his decision was made. Years before, while the President was still a Representative, he boarded a crowded street car, and took the last empty seat. An elderly lady carrying a heavy burden entered the car. She walked its length, but no one offered her a seat. She paused by a seat in which sat one of the men the President later considered for an appointment. This man adjusted his newspaper so that he could not see the woman. McKinley arose and asked the woman to occupy his seat. The man never knew that his act, which he thought would be unnoticed, later prevented his attaining what might have been considered the crowning achievement of his career. So much may hang on so little; and it is this fact which should make all Christians extremely careful to avoid giving offence to any other person.

" I Taught Him To Do It "

I shall not easily forget the heart-broken mother who asked me to pray for her wayward son. " Mr. Powell," she sobbed, " please pray for my boy. He is a slave to gambling. All his wages, all he possesses is being lost. He has a lovely wife, but oh, sir, he is ruining everything by his craving to gamble. He gambles on horses; he gambles on dogs; he gambles on cards. Mr. Powell, please pray for him. I'm breaking my heart."

" Where did he learn to play cards?" I quietly asked. " Did you teach him in your Christian home?" For a few minutes she seemed horribly frightened as the implications of the question reached her soul. Then she whispered, " God forgive me, I taught him to do it."

SAMUEL . . . the boy who saved a nation

(1 SAMUEL 3 : 8-10)

The last worshippers had gone from Shiloh; the shadows of night were falling upon Israel. A boy looked at the golden glow in the western sky, and slowly closed the doors of the sanctuary. Soon it would be bedtime; but before he retired for the night, it would be necessary to attend to the lamp. Yes, it was safe; already the flame was beginning to go out; there could be no danger of fire. Samuel went to his bed and lay down to sleep. How much did he know? Did he remember that Moses had served in this sacred shrine? Did he see again the resolute hands which first placed the lamp in position? Did he know that God had commanded the lamp should never be permitted to go out?

The Lamp Reflecting

What changes had taken place since those days! Then revival fervour had filled the souls of the people, and in response to the commands of God, plentiful supplies of olive oil had been brought to enable the lamp to continue burning. Those blessed days had gone. Now the people were lethargic, and even within the tabernacle all was not well. The lamp hanging before the altar was truly symbolical; the holy flame was dying. Once that great building had been the rallying point in the nation; once its precincts had echoed with the message of God. Now Shiloh was a dead church! The people knew of its existence, but few attended its services. Gone were the soul-thrilling orations given by Moses. Absent were the stirring, joyous dances of the women folk—Shiloh was just another place! Would it be correct to suggest that this is a picture of the modern church? The church has known times when her influence extended to all parts of the nation; when her ministers were prophets indeed; when sinners knelt in the sanctuary to seek and find God. Sometimes even now, in isolated places, it is possible for a moment to obtain glimpses of what used to be; but elsewhere the lamp is going out. Services are uninteresting, sermons are essays, and the monotonous ramblings of the preacher are but an apology for the cry of the ancient prophet whose denunciation of sin made kings tremble.

The Lad Responding

Samuel stood watching the flickering lamp—the lamp in which the heart of the nation was clearly reflected. God had waited for this moment. He remembered the home of strain where a woman, taunted by her jealous rival, had prayed earnestly for a son. Again and again God had refused to answer her petition. She was waiting for a boy; He waited for her. She saw only the nagging rival; He saw the dying nation. And then the waiting time ended, when Hannah promised to surrender her son for service if only God would grant her request. That moment made history. God gave to her the desire of her heart; and remembering to keep her vow, the grateful woman brought her son to the temple. Samuel remained, to " grow up before the Lord." He closed his eyes, and from the shadows came the voice of God. That night gave place to the dawn of a new day, and led to the rescue of a decadent nation. Some things are worthy of consideration. (i) No sin can ever destroy God's interest in His people. (ii) No home is too insignificant for God to visit. (iii) No nation need despair if within its borders God can find a Samuel.

The Lord Returning

Dawn had come. The boy, who seemed to have grown older, moved toward the door. He would never forget the moment when he whispered, " Speak, Lord, thy servant heareth." Neither would he forget that instant when an unseen hand ordained him for a special task. He had a great amount to learn, but at least his path in life had become clear. The door was opened; the light shone in, and the entire proceeding seemed prophetic. Soon it became known that Samuel was established to be a prophet of the Lord. His radiant face, his quiet dignity, his increasing power demonstrated the fact that God was with him; and all Israel watched and wondered. And then the old days returned, for worshippers increased; oil was brought again to the sacred house; the lamp continued to burn. And in many of Israel's homes, people remembered the boy in Shiloh. Probably more than one parent said, " We have no boy to give to God, but at least we can help to train this one," and every year they brought their tithes into God's storehouse, and revival came to Israel. Perhaps God is still looking for a Samuel. Again God may be waiting for a parent to say, " Lord, you can have my son." It might be well for us all to ask, " If the salvation of the world depended upon my readiness to help the Lord, what would happen?"

The Slave Boy

" How much am I bid for him?" The auctioneer was eloquent, but the slave buyers only laughed, for the boy being offered in the Nigerian market was unquestionably ugly. His thin, frightened face had an appalling appearance, and the buyers seriously doubted their ability to find a market for such a lad. The salesman tried again; and when no monetary bid was forthcoming, he sold the slave for a roll of tobacco. Everybody laughed. This was fun, and provided a little amusement amidst the more serious business of buying humans. The new owner took the lad; and other slaves, one by one, were offered to the traders.

Soon, the ugly boy was marching with many other captives along the forest paths which led to the coast. He was careful to keep up with the others, for the merciless traders knew how to use a whip. The journey seemed endless, and sorrow filled his heart. His people and his village were far behind; ahead lay slavery and the unknown. He tramped on. When the sea came into sight, he wondered what new horrors may be awaiting him, and fear again filled his heart when he was pushed aboard a ship and imprisoned in a hold.

Then came a day when people seemed to be running all over the place. Voices were raised; something had gone wrong. British sailors had captured the ship; the evil traders were subdued. The slave vessel was brought into Freetown, where the slaves were set free. The boy was unable to fend for himself, so the authorities placed him in the care of some missionaries. It seemed difficult for the child to believe that these white people could be so kind, when other white people had been so cruel. And the years passed by. The ugly little boy heard about Christ, and ultimately became a Christian. He was sent to school, and through diligent study progressed admirably with his lessons.

Years later came the day when in the presence of great ecclesiastical dignitaries, in St. Paul's Cathedral, London, that same boy was consecrated the first Bishop of Nigeria. The lad who was sold for a roll of tobacco became Bishop Samuel Crowther, who did such a wonderful work for God in Africa. Today he is still lovingly remembered as the man who brought the light of the glorious Gospel to many people. Here was another Samuel, the boy who helped to save a nation.

The Boy Who Fell Out of Bed!

Bump! Unmistakably something was wrong; and mother, greatly alarmed, rushed toward the child's bedroom, to see her youngster sleepily getting to his feet. He had rolled too far to one side of the bed, and the result, for him, seemed catastrophic. The mother placed her arms around the child and asked if he had hurt himself. Reassured that all was well, she tucked him in bed once more; but before she went away, asked, " Son, how did you manage to fall out of bed? " His childlike answer was thought-provoking: " Mum, I suppose I stayed too close to the getting-in side." Perhaps, without knowing it, that boy supplied the answer to many modern Church problems. No thinking person within the Church would ever feel satisfied with the spiritual progress of all who profess faith in the Lord Jesus. Some seem to fall so easily; indeed, they seem to be forever falling. They must be staying so close to the getting-in side of Christianity. Just as each child needs to grow, so every Christian needs to grow in grace, until the babyhood experience has been left far behind, and the convert has grown strong in God. Progress is the password for spiritual growth; without this we remain dwarfs.

The Boy from Inverness

This story cannot be completed; I only know a part. It began in the mid-nineteen-forties, when one Sunday night I preached in the Empire Theatre, Inverness, Scotland. I was conducting an evangelistic crusade in the Baptist Church, but my good friend the Rev. John MacBeath booked the theatre for the Sunday evening. At the conclusion of the service, several people came forward to indicate their desire to become Christians. Nearly thirteen years later, during my mission in Canada, a letter arrived, and the "Red Sea" postmark interested me greatly. I knew no one in that part of the world. When I opened the letter, I read among other things words to this effect, "Dear Mr. Powell, years ago in Inverness, Scotland, at the conclusion of your meeting in the Empire Theatre, one Sunday night, your wife led me to Christ. . . . I am now on my way to northern India to be a missionary. I thought you would like to know. . . ." His story is not yet finished. His name—George MacDonald. His address—158 Purasawelkam High-road, Madras 7, India.

THE INVINCIBLE ANCIENTS . . . and the secret of their power

(1 SAMUEL 31:11-13; 1 CHRONICLES 11:15-19; 3 JOHN 7)

Spiritual enthusiasm is controlled passion; the dynamic which sends weaklings forth to subdue the mighty. Men fired with this rare quality conquer worlds. Today scientists lean over their drawing boards, technicians work overtime, and the resources of great countries are dedicated to the thrilling prospect of sending space-ships to explore the heavens.

Enthusiastic men never admit defeat, and that undoubtedly is the secret of their eventual triumph. Long ago this same quality enabled unlearned men to challenge the might of pagan empires; this unconquerable energy established the Church, and sent missionaries to the end of the earth. In all ages, enthusiasm has been the life of the Church. For a few moments, let us turn back the pages of history.

The Citizen's Challenge . . . on the Walls of Beth-shan—
1 Samuel 31:11-13

It was a dark and shadowy night for the fugitives who lay around the make-shift camp. Far away, upon the field of battle lay the bodies of many comrades, and buried forever were the hopes of Israel. Demoralised and completely vanquished by hordes of Philistines, survivors had fled for their lives. When a sentry whispered a warning, the men became alert; someone was approaching their camp. Then a man staggered into the midst of the watching soldiers, and was recognised as one given up for dead. He told the story of the death of Saul, and how his headless body had been suspended from the walls of the Philistine stronghold; and instantly " the men of Jabesh Gilead arose, and went all night, and took the body of Saul and the bodies of his sons from the wall of Beth-shan. . . ." They remembered how Saul had once been their saviour (1 Samuel 11), and their undying gratitude banished their weakness and turned each man into a giant. They did it for the king's sake!

The Captain's Courage . . . for the Well of Bethlehem—
1 Chronicles 11:15-19

Stealthily, with infinite care, the young man wriggled his way up the face of the hillside. He was in enemy-controlled territory, and one mistake might lead to worse than death. Occasionally he paused, his keen eyes sweeping the surrounding hills. Every tree, every rock was examined for the presence of an enemy; but the whole scene seemed devoid of life. A little farther, and then peering over the highest ridge, the watcher gazed down upon the quaint little town of Bethlehem. Alas, the Philistines were in evidence everywhere. Turning to beckon the others who had quietly followed, the man was soon joined by David and two other captains. Together they watched the intruders in the valley. Suddenly, David sighed and said, " Oh that one would give me drink of the water of Bethlehem, that is at the gate." and even while he was speaking, his faithful captains resolutely made their plans. " And the three brake through the host of the Philistines, and drew water . . . and brought it to David." Perhaps it seemed a foolhardy thing to attempt, but they remembered how David had been their saviour (1 Sam. 22:2) and their enthusiasm made possible the impossible. They did it for the Master's sake!

The Christians' Crusade . . . in the World of Bloodshed—
   3 John 7

The old man John paused, quill in hand, and reminisced. He was writing a short letter to the well-beloved Gaius, but his wandering thoughts had interrupted the task. His mind was going back over the decades; he was remembering colleagues who had long since gone home to heaven. He smiled; yes, they had been wonderful workers. They had vanquished heathen powers, and had triumphed in the greatest cause on earth. He sighed, and returning to his parchment, wrote, ". . . for his name's sake they went forth, taking nothing of the Gentiles." Enthusiasm took the early Christians to market places, to synagogues, to homes, to face the lions, to suffer death by inhuman means. Enthusiasm gave birth to eloquence, and the story of Christ was told everywhere. These early Christians remembered the Cross, and their enthusiasm propelled them into the unknown. Today our world is filled with churches, clergy, and institutions, but something is wrong. We are machines without power; rockets without dynamic; Christians without holy fire. Church deacons throw their hats in the air at a ball game; shy, nervous creatures embrace strangers when their favourite star scores a goal; stammering people possess silver tongues when market prices, weather prospects, or even new fashions are under discussion; but when Christ' name is mentioned— " Shhhhhhhhh! We must not steal the minister's job! Yes, sir, there is a time for everything, and this is Wednesday afternoon, not Sunday morning! Shhhhhhhhh! Turn on the T.V., there might be a mannequin parade coming on! "

Pailo cemetery, near the city of Tacloban, on Leyte Island in the Philippines, was very still. Officers and men of the United States Navy stood silently in long straight lines, and each heart was deeply stirred. The padre, the Rev. William Prigger, was concluding the burial service for 131 men who had been killed when a Japanese Kamikasi (suicide plane) brought devastation and destruction to the U.S. battleship *Nashville*. The men watched and listened, and were conscious of the fact that so easily they too might have died with their comrades. Suddenly the plaintive notes of " Call to Colours " rang out, and the flag which had been flying at half-mast slowly rose to the mast-head. The firing squad had paid their tribute to fallen comrades, and all men stood at the salute. They would never forget that tragic day when destruction hurtled from the skies above the Pacific.

To them, at first, it seemed inconceivable that fanatical Japanese pilots would willingly sacrifice themselves for their Emperor, but their superior officers insisted that this would be the case. Indeed, the suicide flyers would be a menace to all United States ships. When the treacherous attack was launched, the sky seemed filled with planes, and bombs were soon falling everywhere. Then came the screaming sounds of a plane hurtling toward the decks of the battleship, and in the ill-fated moments which followed, 131 men were killed. The wounded were rushed to hospital, where the grim fight to save life continued day and night; but in the quietness of the Pailo cemetery the unfortunate victims of enemy madness were buried with full military honours.

The padre, his task completed, stood back and looked at his boys. They were all impressed; but one young man, Harold Adams, seemed more upset than the rest. His face was intensely grim, and when he was asked the nature of his thoughts during the interment, he replied, " Chaplain, those men died for us." " Yes, I know," answered the padre; " but what do you think we should do about it? " With compelling energy, Adams said, " I don't know what you are going to do, chaplain; I don't know what the other chaps are going to do; but I'll tell you what I intend to do. When the ship is refitted and out on the ocean again; when *General Quarters* is sounded, I'm going back to my battle station. I'll stay at my gun till every enemy plane is shot out of the air, and every enemy ship is sunk to the bottom of the ocean. Yes, I'll stay at my post until that for which these chaps died becomes a reality in this world."

Years later, in October, 1958, when I was welcomed to the city of Edmonton, in Alberta, Canada, I was delighted to discover that the Rev. William Prigger, then the minister of the First Baptist Church, Calgary, had been invited to deliver an address at the inaugural meeting of the evangelistic crusade. I shall never forget the moments when this fine servant of God re-lived his wartime experiences. As he described the Japanese attack, and recalled the burial service for his comrades, he reiterated the sentiments of Harold Adams. Then he spoke of Another, Who died to bring peace to a troubled world. He reminded us of Christ's sacrifice, and asked what we intended to do about the matter. Against the setting of a sailor's determination, Mr. Prigger intimated that each Christian should stay at his post until every evil agency had been swept from the battlefields of life; until each hateful thing in national and international life had been destroyed; until those glorious principles for which Christ died swayed the world.

It was said of the church at Laodicea that its members were neither hot nor cold. They were lukewarm, and as such were quite unacceptable to God. It is difficult to understand how some Christians vow allegiance to Christ and then remain apathetic in regard to the extension of His kingdom. Some desire increasing wealth, and forget that ultimately it can only supply a tomb. Others crave for fame in the realms of sport, and forget that humans have poor memories. Things which are temporal are quickly forgotten. Even empires may arise and fall, to be remembered only by historians. The kingdom of God is eternal; to work for it, to extend its influence, to please its King—these are the greatest achievements in life.

> Christ wants the best. He in the far off ages
>   Once claimed the firstlings of the flock, the finest of the wheat;
> And still He asks His own, with gentlest pleading,
> To lay their brightest hopes, their riches, talents at His feet:
>   He'll not forget the feeblest service, humblest love;
> He only asks that of our store we give to Him
>   The best we have.
> And is our best too much? Ah, friends, let us remember
>   How once our Lord poured forth His soul for us,
> And in the prime of His mysterious manhood
>   Gave up His precious life upon the cross:
> The Lord of Lords, by Whom the worlds were made,
>   Through bitter griefs and tears gave us
>   The best He had.

THREE QUESTIONS . . . which echo across the centuries

(2 SAMUEL 19:34; 1 KINGS 18:21; REVELATION 6:11)

Often, in the presentation of truth, it is advisable to bring together texts which originally belonged to different generations. When these are compared and contrasted, listeners are more equipped to understand the teaching of Holy Scripture. It is proposed in this study to illustrate the fact by joining three verses which reach across the centuries.

How Long have I to Live?

David and his faithful friend Barzillai travelled side by side along the dusty highway; both were silently reminiscent, for much had happened in recent days. Insurrection had been overcome, and the evil schemings of Prince Absalom had been completely destroyed. Triumphantly, the king now returned to his palace; but he was destined to remember for ever the old man who had been his stay in the time of trouble. David was grateful, and planned to take his friend to the royal city. "And the king said unto Barzillai, Come thou over with me, and I will feed thee with me in Jerusalem. And Barzillai said unto the king, How long have I to live . . . I am this day fourscore years old . . . Let thy servant, I pray thee, turn back again, that I may die in my own city, and be buried by the grave of my father and of my mother." He recognised that soon would come the summons to appear in an even greater palace, and the necessity of retiring to the privacy of his own home where preparation could be made for the supreme moment in his life. "How long have I to live?" Every soul should ask that question. Barzillai could teach us much, for in these modern times we seem to have lost the wisdom of the ancients. We live for the transient pleasures of time; they thought of the eternal, saw the invisible, and grasped reality.

How Long Halt Ye between Two Opinions?

From the distance, Carmel looked like a mammoth ant-hill. Vast crowds covered the mountain, and seething excitement filled every heart. Elijah had returned! The man whose word had closed the heavens; the prophet who had been sought in vain; the saint upon whose head the king had put a price: Elijah the elusive had returned. "And Elijah came unto all the people, and said, How long halt ye between two opinions? if the Lord be God, follow him: but if Baal, then follow him. And the people answered him not a word." They heard his challenge, watched the preparation of the altar, and probably joined in the supplication to Baal; but all the while they realised that Jehovah alone could solve their problems. That day they faced their greatest challenge. All around the parched countryside needed water. The entire nation seemed to be dying, and unless relief were forthcoming, all hope of survival could be abandoned. Knowing this, Elijah presented his immortal challenge. If he were present today, he would probably use identical words. The fear of war is heavily upon the nations; homes and communities are being spoiled through sin. Slowly we drift toward calamity. We cry to God when danger threatens; we forget Him when it is gone. We seem to be expert at turning around on the top of a fence. The need of this hour is that men should solemnly consider the facts, and supply an answer to the question asked by the prophet's text.

How Long, O Lord . . . dost Thou not Judge?

From his prison on the isle of Patmos, John was transported in thought to see " the things which should be hereafter," and when in later days he described his experience, he wrote, " I saw under the altar the souls of them that were slain for the word of God, and for the testimony which they held: and they cried with a loud voice, saying, How long, O Lord, holy and true, dost thou not judge and avenge our blood on them that dwell on the earth? . . . and it was said unto them that they should rest for a little season. . . ." Some things are made obvious by this verse. (i) Men deserved judgment. Their guilt was undeniable; they had slain the people of God. (ii) Yet God was reluctant to pour out His wrath. His " little season " suggested that judgment should be delayed. The final description is so terrifying that it becomes easy to understand why God graciously desired to extend to the last possible moment the offer of salvation. " And the kings of the earth, and the great men, and the rich men, and the chief captains, and the mighty men, and every bondman, and every freeman, hid themselves in the dens and in the rocks of the mountains; and said . . . Fall on us, and hide us from the face of him that sitteth on the throne, and from the wrath of the Lamb: for the great day of his wrath is come; and who shall be able to stand? " (Rev. 6:15-17). God's meteorological office gives warning of the approach of a great hurricane. Happy will be the man who finds a safe refuge before the storm breaks.

The Shocking Will

He was rather rugged, a bit blunt, but a good friend for all that. I had known him for several years, and had cause to be grateful for assistance which he had rendered on several occasions. More often than not I went to him for help, for he was an accomplished workman; yet on the day of which I now speak, he came to me. He seemed thoughtful, and I wondered what could have happened. When he was comfortably seated in my home, I asked what I could do for him; and he replied, " Parson, I want you to help me make a will." I answered, " Certainly. Are you thinking of dying? "

" No, parson; but you can never tell, and I want things to be in order."

When he produced the official forms, I filled in the necessary preliminaries, and then commenced writing down the things he dictated. He had thought of everybody. With great care and deliberation he outlined what he desired each member of his family to inherit, and when he had finished dictating his wishes, he exclaimed, " That's the lot." I repeated all that he had stated, and when I had finished, he added, " Parson, that's perfect. You didn't miss a thing. Good." I signed his document, and as I handed it back, asked a question.

" How much will you have? "

He seemed a little bewildered, and it became necessary to explain my question. " Well," I said, " you have made provision for each member of your family. They will all have so much. I wondered how much you will have? " It was difficult to hide my mirth, for as he stared into my face he was utterly bewildered, and obviously wondered if I had taken leave of my senses. Finally he managed to say, " Parson, don't be silly. How can I have anything? I'll be *dead*."

" Yes, I know. Of course you will be dead. You have made provision for all the relatives left behind in this world. Have you made any for yourself in the world to which you will be going? When I go overseas, I send money in advance so that I shall not arrive penniless. Have you sent anything into eternity? Will you be bankrupt there, or—well, tell me friend, *How much will you have?* "

Suddenly he understood what I meant, and as his shoulders sagged, he said, " Good God, I never thought about that." His attitude seems to be very widespread. We think of every eventuality in life except the most important one. We plan for years of progress; we envisage having unlimited time to expend on pursuits of pleasure, and yet—How long have we to live?

The Strange Refusal

During the autumn of 1958, Canadians throughout the country talked of the sad case of a young lad who had accidentally shot himself. He was rushed to hospital, where

doctors declared him to be in urgent need of blood transfusions. Alas, the boy's parents belonged to a movement
where transfusions were considered evil. Increasing pressure
was brought to bear upon the adamant parents, but they
refused to reconsider their decision. Suggestions were made
in high legal circles that new laws be passed immediately to
authorise the transfusions, for arteries had been severed and
the boy was obviously dying. Delay followed delay, and
finally the news reached the nation that the lad was dead.
This was nothing short of a tragedy, especially since the
parents had made the decision which was to deprive another
of his life. Many Canadians were incensed; yet a similar
mistake was being repeated a million times all over the country. Sinners were dying; their own hope seemed to be a
transfusion of divine energy. Alas, many people even believed
this fact, and yet postponed the operation. *"Now* is the
accepted time; *now* is the day of salvation."

The Man who kept on Living

"How long, O Lord . . . dost thou not judge . . . the
earth?" Probably the greatest of all illustrations dealing
with the magnitude of God's mercy comes from the Scriptures. Certain critics have expressed their inability to believe
that Methuselah lived to be nine hundred and sixty-nine years
of age (Gen. 5:27). I quote from *Bible Treasures,* pages 3
and 4, "The child was named Methuselah. Many and varied
interpretations of this strange name have been given. Certain
scholars have declared that it means ' Man of the dart, or
javelin.' Yet another startling suggestion is that the name
means ' It shall not come till he die ' (Lange's commentary).
. . . It is even more startling to notice that the prediction was
fulfilled . . . in the year of his death, the great flood devas-
tated the earth. . . . But Methuselah lived on and on. Possibly
some men thought he would never die. . . . Yet we know now
that the length of the patriarch's life was an indication of
the overwhelming mercy of God. The homecall of the aged
man would coincide with the closure of the offer of mercy
to a guilty world. Thus he was allowed to linger. In this
instance, God's ' *little while* ' lasted over nine hundred years.
How great is the mercy of God."

HEZEKIAH . . . who made the dust fly

(2 CHRONICLES 29:3-5)

The temple was closed; its only occupants were spiders, mosquitos, and probably a few cockroaches. They were having a field day! King Ahaz had ". . . shut up the doors of the house of the Lord, and made him altars in every corner of Jerusalem " (2 Chron. 28:24). The faithful saints in Israel either worshipped at home or in some secluded place in the mountains. And then Hezekiah came to the throne.

Spring-Cleaning in the House of God—2 Chronicles 29:5

" And Hezekiah said unto the priests, Here me, ye Levites, sanctify now yourselves, and sanctify now the house of the Lord God of your fathers, and carry forth the filthiness out of the holy place. For our fathers have trespassed. . . ." Within a matter of hours from the time of the king's edict, the spiders were running for their lives, and cobwebs were being destroyed by the score. Neglect had given birth to dirt, and since God would never dwell in a filthy shrine, it became necessary for Hezekiah to cleanse the sacred house. Finally the cleaners said, " Moreover all the vessels, which King Ahaz in his reign did cast away in his transgression, have we prepared and sanctified, and, behold, they are before the altar of the Lord." It is worthy of consideration that in this ancient cleansing of the temple, certain things had to be removed, whilst others had to be reclaimed. Defilement had to be banished; holiness had to be restored. Many years later Paul declared, " Know ye not that ye are the temple of God, and that the Spirit of God dwelleth in you? . . . the temple of God is holy, which temple ye are " (1 Cor. 3:16, 17). When a man begins to backslide, the sacred things of the Spirit begin to disappear from his life. Restoration can never be complete until all these priceless jewels are restored to their place before the altar of God.

Sacrificing in the House of God—2 Chronicles 29:20-24

" And the priests went into the inner part of the house of the Lord, to cleanse it, and brought out all the uncleanness which they found in the temple of the Lord into the court of the house of the Lord. And the Levites took it, to carry it out abroad into the brook Kidron " (v. 16). They dropped their rubbish into the brook, and the waters bore it away. Many years later, another Priest stood near the banks of the same little stream. He carried filthiness which He had gathered in many temples; but by the time His plans were

completed, the entire burden—the sin of the whole world—
was swept into oblivion (John 18:1; 1 John 2:2). "Then
Hezekiah the king rose *early*. . . ." All true saints are anxious
to proceed with the task; procrastination is abhorred. First,
the blood of the sin offering for penitence; then the blood of
the burnt-offering for praise was placed upon the altar, and
the way was open for God to visit His people. And although
many centuries have since elapsed, these basic principles
remain unchanged. God is anxious to fill us with His Holy
Spirit; but alas, we do not rise early to go into the temple.
We only enter when our eyes are too tired, and the light is
too dim to see the spiders!

Singing in the House of God—2 Chronicles 29:27-30

"And Hezekiah commanded to offer the burnt-offering
upon the altar. And when the burnt-offering began, the song
of the Lord began also with the trumpets, and with the instruments ordained by David King of Israel. And all the congregation worshipped, and the singers sang, and the trum-
peters sounded . . . and the king and all that were present
with him, bowed themselves and worshipped . . . and they
sang praises with gladness." Three vital facts sum up the
story. (i) *A sincere repentence.* These people recognised
that they had sinned against God. Blessed by the ministry
of the law and the prophets, they had nevertheless strayed
from the path of righteousness. Their temple was filthy; their
relationships with God strained. They confessed their sin,
and brought offerings. (ii) *A sincere re-dedication.* They
earnestly desired to regain their lost communion, and to walk
again in the paths of blessedness. They bowed humbly before
the altar, and were accepted. (iii) *A triumphant rejoicing.*
Soon the temple was crowded with devout worshippers; the
hearts and homes of Israel became radiant, and the nation
began to lift up its head. The recurring songs of Zion broadcast the fact that "The Lord, he is God."

> Cleanse me from my sin, Lord,
> Put Thy power within, Lord;
> Take me as I am, Lord,
> And make me all Thine own:
> Keep me day by day, Lord,
> Underneath Thy sway, Lord;
> Make my heart Thy palace,
> And Thy royal throne.

"I Stole your Pig"

One of the most stirring chapters in the history of overseas
missions is now being written in the Central Highlands of
New Guinea. The threat of enemy invasion made it necessary

for the Australian Government to send troops to offset this threat, and it was this expeditionary force which took the Australian Baptist chaplains, for the first time, into "the land that time forgot." Hidden among the towering hills of this strange land, tribes of natives were found who were not known even to exist. They were primitive Stone Age people, who still fought with bows and poisoned arrows. When the padres returned to their homeland they carried the new challenge, and as a result of their indomitable efforts the Baptist Church in Australia established a new mission field.

The work was exceedingly difficult; the language presented problems of considerable magnitude. Yet the work advanced from the simplest of beginnings, and eventually the base station and a few out-stations were proclaiming the glad news of the Gospel. Sometimes it was difficult to assess the real progress of the endeavour, for without adequate knowledge of that particular native tongue it was difficult to ascertain whether or not the people understood. The first requests for baptism were deliberately side-stepped, lest a too premature confession of faith from former heathen should react unfavourably on the work. However, there came a time when the baptismal service could no longer be postponed, and arrangements were made for seven to confess their faith in Christ. By the time the awaited day arrived, this number had increased to forty-seven; and before that day was over, amazing things had taken place within the Baiyer River Valley.

The native people spontaneously met in a holy assembly, for many of them felt compelled to reveal hidden sins. They had not been instructed to do this; but as their desire to become Christians deepened, their consciousness of sin similarly increased. When they met together, one man confessed he had secretly stolen a pig from a neighbour; he paid his debt by returning another pig. Others confessed they had defrauded people in one way or another, and the debt was paid in cash or kind. And as the power of God fell upon that dusky assembly, tears commenced to roll on many faces. Obviously the deepest heart-searching ever to reach the tribes was producing phenomenal effects. The missionaries calmly watched and thanked God. Then came the request from the people, that others not yet prepared for baptism should be permitted to form a procession and walk to the baptismal pool, in order to confess to the thousands of onlookers that they also wished to become Christians. This permission was granted, but even the missionaries were amazed when one thousand men and women lined up to march solemnly to the riverside. It was wonderful; it was thrilling; it was the work of God.

During the months which followed the memorable day, the work increased in strength; and eventually native churches were formed, and native pastors appointed. The initial vision of the wartime padres had become a reality; Christ had come to the Baiyer River districts, and the light of the glorious Gospel was shining brightly where once the darkness of heathenism had prevailed. Yet as in retrospect the Baptists of Australia review the entire project, it is manifest that the turning point from hard struggle to glorious achievement came, when on their own initiative, men and women turned from their evil ways, to clean their lives, and transform their souls into sanctuaries. The work in New Guinea has grown almost beyond recognition, and today people who not so very long ago were still cannibals, are turning toward the Christian faith. In the most unlikely places on earth, churches are being established, and the fair Name of the Saviour is being glorified.

Is it too much to believe that similar things could happen in the Western world if our church followed the pattern of the native peoples of New Guinea? Is there a danger that our modern sophistication has filled us with a false pride; that to weep over our sin would be detrimental to our social standing; that to confess our coldness of heart might undermine our influence in high circles of society? Jesus said, " If any man thirst, let him come unto me, and drink . . . and out of his inner man shall flow rivers of living water." Every Christian could be a channel, to carry the life-giving flow to needy people. Alas, so often, and so easily, the channels are blocked by sin. We all pray for revival; but the key to its coming rests, not with God, but with the people God is waiting to use.

NEHEMIAH . . . a man concerned

The beginning and the end of this book of Nehemiah are in striking contrast. At the beginning, we find a contented Hebrew whose temple is in ruins. At the end, we find the same Hebrew, his hands grimy, his face lined with care; but his sanctuary is resplendent. The message of this book might be applied in two ways. It is possible to think of God's city as represented by the Church, where, alas, there seems to be a cold disregard of spiritual things. On the other hand, we may think of the sanctuary in the hearts of God's children; that temple in the soul where the glory and power of God may not be as evident as the Lord would desire. The former is important; but if revival comes to the Church, God must send it. The revival in the individual heart is our responsibility, and should be our first concern. God may build the universal Church, but we are required to help. *God may create stone, but He never makes a quarry. The Lord may supply the necessary requisites, but He never mixes cement!* Certain tasks must inevitably be ours!

Consider His Prosperity

Nehemiah was a man who had every reason to be proud of himself. Admittedly he was a captive in an alien land, but even there he had advanced to stand in the king's presence. The ancient record reveals how he was held in high esteem, and was able to find favour with his illustrious master. Yet there is no evidence that prosperity had ruined his faith. On the contrary, there is reason to believe that if meetings were ever held in Babylon, this cup-bearer would have been present. He was no blatant idolator; he never bowed before an idol. Had he been examined regarding his theological outlook, he would have passed with honours. His danger came from lack of concern, a dreamy complacency, a complete absence of that spiritual passion which makes dwarfs giants! His temple had fallen into a state of disrepair, while he remained at ease. His soft, smooth hands matched the mood of his soul—until his complacency was suddenly shattered. Then he realised that something was wrong. Let it be admitted that only very strong saints can offset the challenge of prosperity. England was seldom closer to God than when enemy bombs were falling upon her cities. Need is the siren which sends a warning through the souls of men.

Consider His Pain

When he heard, " The remnant that are left of the captivity there in the province are in great affliction and reproach: the wall of Jerusalem also is broken down, and the gates thereof are burned with fire," he wept, mourned, fasted and prayed before the God of heaven. Wonderful indeed are the tears which arise from a contrite heart. Blessed are those eyes which see and weep over the desolation of God's property. God may speak in the mind; but He dwells in the heart. Unless His glory shines from that sanctuary, even the most potent message is but an echo. We might well enquire if our walls need repair. It might be to our eternal profit to examine every inch of our Christian profession, to ascertain whether or not neglect has undermined our strength.

Consider His Prayer

Suddenly Nehemiah's skies became overcast, and the sun ceased to shine. His prayer deserves consideration, for he said, " Let thine ear now be attentive, and thine eyes open, that thou mayest hear the prayer of thy servant, which I pray before thee now, *day and night,* for the children of Israel thy servants, and confess the sins of the children of Israel, which we have sinned against thee: *both I and my father's house have sinned.* We have dealt very corruptly against thee . . ." (1:6, 7). *A personal responsibility.* Nehemiah identified himself with the sins of other people. He exclaimed, " *we* have sinned." This is the hall-mark of sincerity. Alas, many people condemned by the word of God endeavour to place the blame elsewhere. *A persistent remorse.* His concern reached to the depth of his being. This was not a mood soon to be forgotten: he had sinned, and the consciousness of his guilt continued until he prayed *day and night.* When wounds are deep, prayers are long; when God recognises reality, His hands are quickly outstretched. *A powerful resolve.* The cure for sore knees is to take the weight from them! Tears may remove the dirt from our eyes; they never build walls. Unless our concern be followed by the consecration of our talents to the restoration of the sanctuary, we waste time in praying. Nehemiah saw and accepted a challenge. His glorious example should inspire us as we pick up our tools!

Melanchthon's Parable

When Martin Luther rebelled against the excessive authority of the Pope, and began to oppose the evil practices of his time, there were many other lesser-known people who fully shared his views. Although not in the fore-front of the theological battles which were soon raging in many centres, these men recognised in Luther's outbursts the expression of their own convictions. Melanchthon belonged to this number. Alas, as the reformation gained ground, certain men used the movement to propagate their own narrow teachings, and within a short while even the ranks of the reformers were filled with divisions. Melanchthon deplored the bitterness of the quarrels which followed, and in a supreme endeavour to make his contemporaries recognise the danger of their discontent, wrote a parable. He said, " There was a war between the wolves and the dogs. The wolves sent out a spy, to see how best they could defeat the dogs. Returning, the spy said, ' If we just leave them alone, they will defeat themselves. There are so many different kinds of dogs, one can hardly count them; and as for the worst of them, they are mostly little dogs who do a lot of barking but cannot bite. However, this I did observe and I could clearly see, that while they all hated us wolves, yet each dog suspected every other, and were constantly fighting each other." The wolf was right; the dogs defeated themselves."

Many years have passed since the reformer wrote his strange parable, yet we could almost believe that he wrote it yesterday. Everywhere the cause of God seems to be in ruins; the churches are comparatively empty, and only the few faithful people in Zion seem to care. Here and there around the world people pray for revival, and the most ardent souls yearn for the time when a modern Nehemiah will arise to restore the blessedness to Zion. Alas, the greatest enemy to a spiritual revival is the Church herself. It is problematical whether the Church is ever more untruthful than when she sings enthusiastically—

> Like a mighty army
>   Moves the Church of God;
> Brothers, we are treading
>   Where the saints have trod.
> *We are not divided,*
>   All one body we,
> *One in hope, in doctrine,*
>   One in charity.

The divisions now existing within the Church of God, and even within those sections supposedly evangelical are sufficient to break the heart of God. Melanchthon's parable is as applicable today as it was in his own time.

The first recorded prayer of Nehemiah suggests that he had much practise in the noble art of intercession. The pitiable condition of Jerusalem only supplied the sombre setting against which Nehemiah's petitions shone forth as stars. His first prayer was, " I beseech thee, O Lord of heaven, the great and terrible God, that keepeth covenant and mercy for them that love him and observe his commandments: let thine ear now be attentive, and thine eyes open, that thou mayest hear the prayer of thy servant, which I pray before thee now, day and night. . . ."

He Prayed for His Life!

Editor M. R. De Haan tells the entrancing story of a British soldier who was caught one night creeping stealthily back to his camp. He had been in some nearby woods, and his actions were sufficient to arouse the gravest suspicion. Paraded before his commanding officer, he was required to explain his movements; and thereupon explained that he had visited the woods in order to pray. That was his only defence. The officer suspected that this was but an excuse for a flagrant violation of camp rules, and growled, "Have you been in the habit of spending hours in private prayer?"

"Yes, sir."

"Then down on your knees and pray now," the officer roared; "you never needed to pray as much as you do now."

Expecting immediate death, the soldier knelt and poured out his soul in earnest prayer; and as the officer listened, he recognised reality. This man had surely prayed often; otherwise he could not have become eloquent at a moment's notice. When the prayer was finished, the commander said, "You may go. I believe your story. If you hadn't drilled often, you could not have done so well at review."

> Prayer is the soul's sincere desire,
> Uttered or unexpressed;
> The motion of a hidden fire
> That burns within the breast.

NEHEMIAH . . . a man constrained

Something was wrong! The animated, joyous butler was stricken by sorrow. The sparkle had gone from his eyes; his movements were listless. The king watched his servant; yes, something was wrong! "Wherefore the king said unto me, Why is thy countenance sad, seeing thou art not sick? this is nothing else but sorrow of heart." And Nehemiah trembled. His sun was in eclipse; a chill of fear sent dread through his soul. The business of restoring a sin-sick sanctuary was never easy!

How Weak

We do well to consider that the task confronting this butler was far too great for a man of his type. It was inconceivable that a slave should build a city. Vast quantities of materials had to be supplied, considerable sums of money would be required, and numerous craftsmen employed to complete the task. The whole project seemed ridiculous. Nehemiah was a wise man; he ceased looking at the difficulties, and turned his eyes heavenward. Sometimes the longest way around is the shortest way home! With men, certain things are impossible; but with God, all things are possible. Nehemiah's quick prayer, his exceeding great requests, his undeniable passion to rebuild God's city, revealed the fact that for him nothing else mattered. He had put his hand to a plough; he could not look back.

How Willing

The night was still; the city ruins, ugly and grotesque in the moonlight, were monuments to the savagery of bygone days. The scene was utterly desolate as Nehemiah moved between the piles of fallen masonry. The tragic news which had reached him in Babylon had been an under-statement. The position beggared description; but this was no time for tears. Nehemiah squared his shoulders and went to challenge the elders; and God was with him. Soon, the son of one of the chemists had commenced building. Probably his hands became sore and grimy, but his heart was singing. Not far away, one of the rulers had put aside his robes of office; his working clothes revealed he was still a *man*. Among the men laboured the daughters of yet another ruler, and never were Old Testament women seen in a better light. Eliashib the high priest put God first, and was paid double rate! See *Bible Cameos*, page 67. The fact that the nobles put not their necks to the work should make us search our hearts, lest their descendants be hiding there!

How Worrying

Rome was not built in a day; neither was any other city! The restoration of a ruined sanctuary is not a sudden decision made at the communion table. It is not the inspiring flash of resolution thrilling the soul in a consecration meeting. This is a crusade; a holy effort leading to struggle, bitter resolve, tears, perspiration, and perhaps blood. Sometimes a wise builder will see the need to make haste slowly. He will build faster by digging deeper! Rubbish was never a good foundation for a church steeple; broken vows were never able to support a sanctuary reaching to the sky. Soon the whispers of criticism became shouts of scorn, "What do these feeble Jews? . . . will they revive the stones out of the heaps of rubbish which are burned? . . . if a fox go up, he shall even break down their stone wall" (4:2, 3). Several items may be listed as rubbish. David's rubbish covered illicit love affairs. Demas had to face the challenge of worldliness; Achan saw his temple crash because of secret sins. It is very dangerous to stand beneath toppling walls!

How Watchful

"They which builded on the wall, and they that bare burdens, with those that laded, every one with one of his hands wrought in the work, and with the other hand held a weapon" (4:17). The builders had both hands occupied; *there was no third hand!* With one hand they erected the wall; with the other they preserved their work. Their great task was sufficient to keep both hands occupied; *they had no fingers for other pies!* To change the simile, some builders have many irons in the fire, but none ever got hot! No man can be effective in God's work if the multitudinous nature of his duties runs him off his feet. The minister who is too busy to linger in the holy place may increase his popularity, but his soul becomes parched. The preacher who spends his week running between Dan and Beersheba will seldom visit the holy mount. Sermons hastily thrown together on a Saturday night resemble dry hash; they are very difficult to digest.

Sunday Morning Sickness

Spiritual enthusiasm on a Sunday morning is a rare jewel. Some years ago a Detroit newspaper printed the following prayer: "Almighty God, as I lie here on this sofa this Sunday morning, surrounded by the Sunday newspapers, and half listening to one of the radio preachers, it has come to me that I have lied to Thee and to myself. I said I did not feel well enough to go to church. That was not true. I was not ambitious enough. I would have gone to the office had it been Monday. I would have played golf had it been Wednesday afternoon. I would have gone to a picture show had it been Friday night. But it is Sunday morning, and Sunday illness covers a multitude of sins. God have mercy on me. I have lied to Thee. I was only lazy and indifferent!"

When I was a student, my studies often kept me out of my bed until two or even three o'clock in the morning. It became my common practice to study until that late hour, and then to sleep for a short while before going to work in the coal-mine. Consequently when Sunday arrived, I was tired and stayed in bed until lunch-time. One day I asked one of the church girls to write something in my autograph album, and undoubtedly desiring to cure my bad habit, she wrote a new verse for " Stand up, stand up for Jesus "—

> Get up, get up for Jesus,
>   Ye soldiers of the cross:
> A lazy Sunday morning
>   Means certain harm and loss.
> The church bells call to worship,
>   In duty be not slack;
> You cannot fight the good fight
>   By lying on your back!

He Desired Grape Juice

B. I. Davidson, a missionary in India, told a thrilling story of one of his native evangelists who came for the first time to visit the city of Calcutta. The man had saved the equivalent of ten dollars, and seemed excited as he accompanied his friend to see the sights. Together they visited the bazaars, and examined the treasures offered for sale. They went into great buildings, and saw many things which amazed the inexperienced visitor. Yet all the while the missionary wondered what the Indian would purchase with his savings. When the tour was almost completed, the evangelist gave the money to Mr. Davidson, saying, " Please buy as much grape juice as you can, so that we shall have enough wine for the communion for many months to come." He could have asked for clothing, shoes, anything; but his delightful request indicated his greatest interest lay in the work of his church. Within his heart burned a fire, and he was determined it should never go out.

The Negro's Secret

A negro minister was once asked the secret of his power. He thought for a moment and then replied, " I reads myself full; I thinks myself clear; I prays myself hot; and then I lets go." It would be a most challenging task if we were asked to decide the order of importance with these four phases. Some people speak for thirty minutes and with compelling eloquence say nothing! Descendants of Solomon, they have no need " to read themselves full." Others, who are always too busy to think, are experts at leading congregations into a fog! " *I prays myself hot.*" Naturally he had to " let himself go," or *he might have burst!* I shall always remember the bitterly cold Sunday afternoon in the north of Scotland when I complained to the stolid elder of the Presbyterian church. Outside, the snow lay deep on the ground; inside the building was no heating apparatus. My teeth were chattering when I said, " Brother, it is very cold in this church." " Yes," he replied, *" we always get our heat from the pulpit."*

Yet another Negro preacher in the Southern States of America was asked how he planned and delivered his sermon. His quaint reply deserves consideration. " First, I expoundulates the Word. Then I illustrifies the point. Finally, *I makes the arousement.*" In this modern age, many sincere people are asking if it is wise to sacrifice enthusiasm upon the altar of refinement. We seem to get enthusiastic about everything except the Gospel. When I hear people objecting to the urgency in the preacher's message, I wonder if the critics would speak in whispers to warn a man about to fall to his death. It is written that God originally kindled the blaze upon the altar at Shiloh. Afterward it became the sacred duty of the priests to keep the fires burning. It is well that we should consider the implication of the ancient Scripture.

O Thou who camest from above
The pure celestial fire to impart,
Kindle a flame of sacred love
On the mean altar of my heart.

There let it for Thy glory burn
With inextinguishable blaze
And trembling to its source return,
In humble prayer and fervent praise.

Jesus, confirm my heart's desire
To work and speak and think for Thee;
Still let me guard the sacred fire,
And still stir up Thy gift in me.

NEHEMIAH . . . a man controlled

Every true revival rests upon the Word of God. One may not always be sure of the methods to be used, nor of the type of instrument to be chosen; but it is indisputable that each time God's people have been brought to heights of spiritual triumph, the Bible has regained its place of authority. The rebuilding of Jerusalem was of paramount importance; but unless the completed task were supported by the radiant living of the builders, the walls would fall once again into a state of disrepair. Revivals can never last unless their foundations go deep into the will of God.

God's Day had to be kept Holy!

" And all the people gathered themselves together as one man into the street that was before the water gate; and they spake unto Ezra the scribe to bring the book of the law of Moses . . . and he read therein . . . from the morning until midday . . . And Ezra opened the book in the sight of all the people . . . and when he opened it, all the people stood up. And Ezra blessed the Lord, the great God. And all the people answered, Amen, Amen, with lifting up their hands: and they bowed their heads, and worshipped the Lord with their faces to the ground " (8:1-6). Every day the people came to receive guidance from the sacred book; and as long as this practice continued, great gladness rested upon the community. We need to learn from their example, and recognise that spiritual health is only maintained by daily contact with the Word of God. " In those days saw I in Judah some treading wine presses on the sabbath . . . and I testified against them " (13:15; cf. 10:31). The man who honours God's day respects God's wishes, and seeks daily to be well-pleasing to Him. This is the hall-mark of revival. The Christian who journeys from Jerusalem to Jericho will soon get a heartache—and a headache too!

God's Tithe had to be Brought

It may be easy for a man whose income goes into the higher wage bracket to tithe, but the people of Nehemiah's day were for the most part exceedingly poor. If ever men could have argued against the requirements of the law, the inhabitants of Jerusalem could have done so. Yet it is worthy of note that the people whose hearts had been revived, never thought of argument. They recognised their indebtedness to

God; they saw the need for means to maintain the service of the sanctuary, and although they were very poor indeed, a tenth of all they possessed was willingly laid at the feet of the Lord (see 10:34-39). A religion unable to reach the depths of a pocket is superficial and useless. An increased offering was insufficient—God asked for a tenth of what He supplied; and when His people failed to honour their obligations, He accused them of being thieves. " Will a man rob God? Yet ye have robbed me. But ye say, Wherein have we robbed thee? In tithes and offerings. . . . Bring ye all the tithes into the storehouse, that there may be meat in mine house, and prove me now herewith, saith the Lord of hosts, if I will not open you the windows of heaven, and pour you out a blessing that there shall not be room enough to receive it " (Mal. 3:8-10). If God permitted a tithing Christian to be financially embarrassed, He would lose His character. Sacrificial giving opens windows in heaven, for God says, " Give, and it shall be given unto you."

God's People had to be Separate

It would appear that the command, " Be not unequally yoked together with unbelievers," was as important in ancient days as it should be today. Many Christians are violating the commands of God in regard to this important matter. It is written that the people under Nehemiah's control made a covenant saying, ". . . we will not give our daughters unto the people of the land, nor take their daughters for our sons " (10:30). Young people should study this chapter before they marry unbelievers; businessmen should heed the command before they become linked with others in bonds which are not pleasing to God. An unholy alliance in business might lead to increasing wealth; an attractive husband or wife might lead to momentary joy; but it is not possible to remain truly happy in one's relationship with God when the commandment is being broken. The people of old recognised these important facts, and bowed down before the will of God. Thus He was able to pour His blessing upon them, and soon ". . . the joy of Jerusalem was heard even afar off."

The Holy Bonfire

During my visit to Winnipeg, Canada, I had the good fortune to meet the Rev. Cyril Hunt who, prior to the Communist seizure of China, worked as a missionary with the China Inland Mission. This devoted servant of Christ was chairman of the committee that organised my evangelistic services, and I shall ever be grateful to him and his colleagues for the magnificent way in which they supported their visiting preacher. Mr. Hunt was a man of wide experience, and anticipating that he might have thrilling stories of China, I asked if he could remember any occasion when a Chinese church was stirred greatly by the power of the Holy Spirit. He thought about my question, and later handed to me a piece of paper upon which he had written a few notes about Mr. Wang.

The Rev. Timothy Lui had been brought from Chekiang Province on the east coast to conduct evangelistic services in Central China. He was an acceptable preacher, and everywhere he ministered churches were helped. After one of his appeals for conversion and re-dedication, between twenty and thirty souls stepped forward to confess their faith in Christ. Mr. Wang was among the number. He was troubled; his conscience urged that he had failed his Lord. This young Chinese Christian owned a hardware business, and had been fairly prosperous; but the entry of Japanese troops into his province provided temptation, to which Mr. Wang succumbed. Dispensing with his normal commodities, he began selling liquor and alcohol, and soon greatly increased his profits. Mr. Wang prospered, but at the expense of his soul. The sermon that evening reminded him of his folly, and greatly disturbed, he resolved to re-dedicate himself to the service of Christ.

This man was so well known that soon everyone knew what had taken place. The following night, when Cyril Hunt was leading the community singing, the local minister asked permission to give a testimony. There was silence when he confessed he had failed his Master. As the tears streamed down his face, he said that Mr. Wang's repentence had revealed a similar need in his own soul. Turning again to the song leader, he asked if they could go out into the church courtyard and continue their service in the open air. Mr. Hunt led the congregation outside, where they stood in a circle; and it was then that the great bonfire was lit. Mr. Wang and his widowed mother brought baskets of cigarettes and large quantities of wine. Other inflammable materials were gathered, and soon the fire was blazing. Mr. Hunt confessed that this was the greatest fire he had ever seen; and the wonderful repercussions which followed stirred the entire city of Wuhu. At one stroke Mr. Wang destroyed his prospects of becoming wealthy. The coming of the Japanese soldiers opened a new field of trading for this young Christian, but realising his soul was becoming sinful, Wang renounced it all. The following night, when the preacher appealed for souls, the front of the church was inadequate to provide room for those who responded. Hundreds of men and women tearfully confessed the desire to surrender to the Lord Jesus Christ. Where people could kneel they did so, to ask God's forgiveness; others stood in corners, around the platform, and wherever they could find room. The power of God flooded the church, and revival became the daily experience of the assembly. One man had cleansed his temple, and the ensuing consecration brought a new Pentecost to the people.

This method has always been the highway to revival. It is possible to organise special meetings, to spend great sums of money on advertising, to expect a visiting evangelist to perform miracles. He undoubtedly will do his utmost toward that desired end; but more often than not, will only succeed in breaking his heart. *Revival begins in the house of God.* When the Lord's people begin to recognise their own needs; when sin is confessed and renounced; when God sees that Christians really mean to be completely consecrated, the Church will be in the position to expect anything.

" If my people, which are called by my name, shall humble themselves, and pray, and seek my face, and turn from their wicked ways; then will I hear from heaven, and will forgive their sin, and will heal their land " (2 Chron. 7:14).

THE PATRIARCHS . . . who were busy doing nothing

(Psalm 46:10; Exodus 14:13; 23:11)

The advertising methods of the late Dr. Lionel Fletcher once caused a minor sensation in the stately city of Cape Town, South Africa. When he announced a special meeting for ladies only, he intimated that his topic would be, *"Woman's Greatest Sin."* Many sensationalists attended the service, but were extremely disappointed when Dr. Fletcher declared this sin to be *worry*. He exclaimed, " You worry about this; you worry about that; you worry about everything." Whether or not he was correct in his deductions may be open to debate, but no intelligent person would deny that worry undermines health, mars happiness, and fills homes with tension. It is thrilling to know that the Bible mentions a remedy.

Be Still . . . and know that I am God

Our world has become a place of noise; of ceaseless activity where men are moved to frenzied effort. Alas, many people only pause when they are demoralised and beaten; they stop then in bewilderment, for they know not what to do or where to go next. When disaster looms ahead, fear grips the soul, and humans droop with weariness. Modern philosophy seems to say that if survival depends upon action, then we must work until we drop. There are times when this is proved to be wrong. There are occasions when being still is a divine art; when to be quiet and inactive are degrees of great distinction. Few men can have more trials than those known to David. Psalm 46 reveals the secret of his confidence. He speaks of the greatness of God; he supplies a glorious text; and finally seems to say, " Stop worrying; banish your anxiety; cast your burdens down, and in the absolute knowledge that the Almighty is *your* God, be at rest."

Stand Sill . . . and see the salvation of the Lord

The situation was desperate; fear clutched the hearts of the children of Israel. Already they were beginning to dispute the wisdom of following Moses. They had been carried away by the enthusiasm of a stranger; they had been irresponsible and foolish! Ahead lay the impassable sea; on either side were lofty mountains; and behind, the legions of the mighty Pharoah. Soon, whips would be lashing Hebrew backs; soon chariots would be crushing old people too tired and weary to move from the path, and disaster would overwhelm the nation. ". . . and the children of Israel said unto Moses, Because there were no graves in Egypt, hast thou taken us away to die in the wilderness? wherefore hast thou dealt with us, to carry us forth out of Egypt? Is not this the word that we did tell thee in Egypt, saying, Let us alone, that we may serve the Egyptians? For it had been better for us to serve the Egyptians, than that we should die in the wilderness. And Moses said unto the people, Fear ye not, *stand still,* and see the salvation of the Lord. . . ." We do well to remember that although God may delay His coming, he is never too late to rescue those who trust Him. The well-known story of Israel's deliverance provides the only comment necessary to enhance the importance of this section of our study.

Lie Still . . . and be fruitful

The commandments given by God to Israel were meant to safeguard their happiness. God had much to say concerning their homes, their families, their possessions, and even their lands. Not the least important was the commandment which said, " And six years thou shalt sow thy land, and shalt gather in the fruits thereof: but the seventh year thou shalt let it rest and *lie still;* that the poor of thy people may eat. . . ." Experience taught the ancient farmers that in obeying this command they increased their prosperity. They discovered that the land which was permitted to *lie still* ultimately became increasingly productive.

This undoubtedly is a law of life. The man who never sleeps is on his way to a suicide's grave; the machinery which never stops for an overhaul may be expected to break down. There are times when a man may do most by doing nothing! The crazy rush of our modern world has almost banished the quiet place and the restful soul. Let us remember again the words concerning the potter, and reflect on the fact that the clay was never quite as valuable as when it lay yielded and still in the craftsman's hand. Let us pause and turn our backs on the madding throng. Let us climb our Olivet, and in the solitude *be still,* and God's benediction will turn our hearts into a fruitful garden.

> Lie still, and let Him mould thee:
>   O Lord, I would obey:
> Be Thou the skilful Potter,
>   And I, the yielded clay:
> Bend me, oh bend me to Thy will,
> While in Thy hand I'm lying still.

Opening Doors . . . the new way

The supermarket stores of Canada are an institution. Customers with cute wire-made push-cars wander along the aisles, selecting from innumerable shelves things they desire to purchase; and when this has been completed, the articles are placed on the turn-tables to be carried to the waiting cashier. When the account has been paid, the goods are neatly packed in cardboard containers, and the customer is ready to leave.

My wife had come to the desk; her money had been paid, and the goods placed in my waiting arms. Ahead was the exit—a large glass door. I waited for Mrs. Powell to open that door, but she smiled and said, " Go on."

" Open the door for me. I cannot walk through the glass."

" Go on," she repeated. For a moment I wondered what had happened to her. She made no attempt to help me, and her smiling face suggested she was either expecting the impossible or going crazy! We had only just arrived on the American continent, but she had made the discovery which later explained her reluctance to help her long-suffering husband!

" Go on," she repeated again; " walk through the door and see what happens." I had a shrewd idea what would happen, and since I desired to preserve the appearance of my nose, suggested she should go first. " Walk," she said again, " and the door will open of its own accord." Her confidence increased my interest in that door. In order to approach the exit, every customer had to walk over a panel let into the floor, and obviously beneath that panel were invisible springs which responded to the pressure of a foot. I had never seen anything like this, and I smile now when I recollect the way in which I went back repeatedly to try out the mechanism. The moment I stepped on the panel, the door opened. Sometimes, when a customer had preceded me and the door was closing, the swing was automatically arrested when another foot touched the hidden mechanism. I have never forgotten my introduction to the doors of the supermarkets. They taught truth of superlative worth. Sometimes the path of the Christian is blocked by insurmountable obstacles; the way to freedom is closed. Yet, as in ancient times, God commands, " Speak unto the children of Israel, that they go forward." The march of faith touches hidden springs of divine power; obstacles are removed, and the way to freedom is opened.

The Door That Defied Houdini

During my childhood the name of the master magician, Houdini, was known throughout the world. His performances suggested the supernatural, and some of his exploits were truly amazing. He performed seemingly impossible feats, and even kings and queens became interested in the achievements of the illustrious artist. Yet one story concerning this strange man deserves a little more publicity; it is the account of one of his rare failures.

During an entertainment tour through the British Isles, Houdini boasted he could escape from any gaol; and in one small provincial town his challenge was accepted. He was escorted to a very small prison, the door was closed against him, and he was told to get out if he could. Houdini worked on the lock until he was almost exhausted. His reputation was at stake; his challengers were waiting to see what would happen. Usually only thirty seconds would elapse before the most intricate mechanism yielded to his persuasions. But this time, the infuriating lock refused to spring. Houdini used every device known to him, but finally, and with great disgust, gave up. As he moved back, his foot slipped and he fell against the door. The sudden bump jarred the handle, and the door opened. The magician was astounded, but his challengers only laughed. *The door had never been locked.* All his struggles had been needless; the way to freedom was open, but he did not know it. It has been said that Houdini enjoyed the joke, but we may be assured he never fell for the same trick twice.

We live in times when around the world men do all kinds of things to be saved. They go on long arduous pilgrimages to distant shrines; they fast, and pray for months on end; they pay enormous sums of money in the hope of gaining forgiveness; they do all kinds of things in all kinds of ways: but this is needless. The Lord Jesus Christ said, " I am the door: by me if any man enter in, he shall be saved " (John 10:9). Sometimes we do most by doing nothing; we travel farther by remaining still; we reach higher by kneeling.

THE GRACE OF GOD . . . in the Gospel according to Isaiah

(ISAIAH 30:15-33)

The grace of God has always been greater than human weakness. Man has ever been a changeable creature, for during the passing of time his habits, environment, and all things associated with him have undergone change. Yet in startling contrast has been his attitude toward God. Persistently and consistently throughout the ages, sinful man has resented divine intervention in his way of living; for man prefers to enjoy the pleasures of sin for a season, than to inherit the riches of grace for ever. This chapter provides a striking example of that fact.

The God Who Witnessed

The people were annoyed; the prophet was getting on their nerves. Their countenances were strained as they watched the young man in their midst. Conscious of their animosity, but determined to do his duty, Isaiah lifted up his voice and cried, "Woe to the rebellious children, said the Lord, that take counsel, but not of me . . . that walk to go down to Egypt . . . to strengthen themselves in the strength of Pharaoh . . . Woe . . . woe . . . woe to these people . . . For thus saith the Lord God, the Holy One of Israel; In returning and rest shall ye be saved; in quietness and in confidence shall be your strength: *and ye would not* . . . ye said, No." Few readers will deny the fact that the ancient scene appears to be strangely modern. Long afterward, another Preacher uttered the same message: "How oft would I have gathered you . . . *and ye would not*" (Matt. 23:37).

The God Who Waited

"And therefore will the Lord wait, that he may be gracious unto you, and therefore will he be exalted, that he may have mercy upon you: for the Lord is a God of judgment: blessed are all they that wait for him." If God rejected us as quickly as we reject Him, utter disaster would overwhelm us. The patience of God is a wonderful thing; and this alone will be responsible for the salvation of innumerable people. God still perseveres with sinners when all others have abandoned the task. I shall always remember the lady who appeared annoyed when certain people refused to accept Christ. Yet, when I asked how long it took her to decide, she answered, "Twenty-seven years." God had been very patient with her—she had need to be patient with others.

The God Who Worked

It does not necessarily follow that when God is waiting, He is inactive. "And though the Lord give you the bread of adversity, and the water of affliction, yet shall not thy teachers be removed into a corner any more, but thine eyes shall see thy teachers: and thine ears shall hear a word behind thee, saying, This is the way, walk ye in it, when ye turn to the right hand, and when ye turn to the left." Oftentimes ships are compelled to seek shelter by the force of a sudden gale. Similarly, there are times when God with great deliberation permits the seas of life to become tempestuous. Then, lives seem to be in jeopardy; but even in the unpleasant experiences of life, the purposes of God are fulfilled. Adversity and affliction are unwelcome guests, but the statement that God allows His ministering servants to remain within sight suggests that He waits to hurry to the rescue of any who ask for assistance. The fact that His voice sounds *behind* us suggests that we are travelling in the wrong direction. God says, "Turn around, for *this* is the way."

> God moves in a mysterious way
> His wonders to perform:
> He plants His footsteps in the sea,
> And rides upon the storm.

The God Who Won

The prophetical nature of Isaiah's message presents a harbinger of hope. We know that this utterance will be fulfilled in Israel's destiny; but the same glorious thing can happen to others, for "God is gracious, and full of compassion." Says the prophet, " . . . the ornament of thy molten images of gold: thou shalt cast them away as a menstruous cloth; thou shalt say unto it, Get thee hence. Then shall he give the rain . . . in that day shall *thy cattle feed in large pastures . . . Ye shall have a song, as in the night* when a holy solemnity is kept; and gladness of heart, as when one goeth with a pipe to come into the mountain of the Lord, to the mighty One of Israel " (vv. 22-24; 29,30). The beginning and the end of this study provide a striking contrast. Had God abandoned His effort when the task was only half completed, it would have been a major tragedy. God sees the end from the beginning, and with great patience works toward the ultimate triumph. His grace is superb.

> Grace there is my every debt to pay,
> Grace to wash my every sin away;
> Grace to keep me spotless day by day,
> In Christ for me.

70

Just Waiting

During the year 1909 Dr. Wilbur Chapman visited Australia, and addressed 3000 men in the city of Melbourne. It has been said that his address that day was one of the greatest he ever delivered. *The Southern Cross Mission Souvenir* carried a condensed report of that memorable meeting, and I take the liberty of reproducing Dr. Chapman's final illustration.

" In the city of Chicago one of our young business men came home one day to find that his wife had lost her reason. She had been ailing for weeks and months. The climax came, and she had gone mad. He did what I should like to have done if the wife had been mine. He gave up his business to stand by her side and help her. The neighbours came to him and said, ' You must take your wife away. She frightens our children.' Having sufficient means, he moved to the edge of the city of Chicago and built a splendid house. The neighbours came again and said, ' The shrieks of your wife terrify our households, and you will have to move.' He led them politely to the door and said, ' My property begins at the iron fence, and my obligation is to my wife.' Then the old family doctor came to him and said, 'George, why don't you take your wife down to the mountains of Tennessee? She was born there. Let her dabble in the brook like a child; let her gather wild flowers; let her hear the birds sing, and maybe she will come back.'

" He took her South as suggested, and she dabbled in the brook like a child, cut flowers, and listened to the mountain birds; but the summer passed, and her reason did not return. The gentleman took her in his private car back to his Chicago home heartbroken. He carried her, so frail she was, in his arms up to her room. He put her in bed, and she went to sleep. She slept for fifteen minutes. She had not had a natural sleep like it for a year. He scarcely breathed. She slept for an hour, and then he put his ear down to her lips to hear if her breathing was regular. She slept for two hours, then three, then all the night; and in the morning, just as the light came through the window and kissed her face, she opened her eyes and was herself again. Looking up into his face, she said, ' Where have I been? ' ' Oh,' he replied, as he reached down to cover her face with kisses, ' you have been on a long journey, but you have come home.' ' But where have you been all the time? ' she asked. He answered, ' All the time right by your side. Waiting, waiting, just waiting.' "

I was only a small child when I first heard the story of the drowning of an Indian woman in America. With her son she was swept away in the flood waters; but she might have been saved if she had not been so terrified. The young man was a strong swimmer, and did all within his power to calm and save his mother. However, she was exceedingly frightened, and each time the water swept across her face, panicked and struggled desperately. Again and again the son regained his hold upon her clothing, but as the struggle continued, he began to lose his strength and was forced to leave her. With great difficulty he dragged himself ashore, where he wept and said, " Oh mother, I could have saved you, but you wouldn't let me."

The Greatness of Grace

Grace is one of the great words of Scripture, and preachers in every age have tried to define it. The dictionary declares that "grace" is divine favour; but Christians will readily acknowledge that this meagre definition is inadequate. Perhaps it is best expressed through an acrostic. G..R..A..C..E. *G*reat *R*iches *A*t *C*hrist's *E*xpense. The boundless mercy of God is now within reach of a sinner, for like Jacob's ladder, the Cross of Christ has made it possible for man to reach the hitherto inaccessible. The limitless wealth of the Eternal may now enrich impoverished people.

I cannot mention his name, for if I did he would be very displeased. He was a saint who loved helping others. He took a penniless boy off the street, fed and clothed him, and taught him the business. He became a father to the young fellow, and the years passed by. Then came the time when the young man separated himself from his friend, and within yards, opened another shop in direct opposition. Undercutting prices, he stole the trade, and brought his "father" to the edge of ruin. However, the boy broke first, and was destitute. Then he was taken back into the old home and forgiven. That was *grace*—grace that had been placed in a human heart by the God of grace.

THREE SERMONS . . . which said the same thing

(ISAIAH 30:15; MATTHEW 23:37; 22:3)

It has been affirmed continually that the Bible is *one book*. From time to time the local colour of varying scenes may appear to change, but the broad underlying principles of the Scripture are always in harmony. Sometimes identical statements may be found centuries apart, and the replica seems to be a bridge across the ages. About 700 B.C. God sent Isaiah to say, " Come now, and let us reason together," but the people " *would not come.*" When Christ looked at the city of Jerusalem, He said, " How oft would I have gathered you . . . and *you would not come.*" One of the greatest of the Saviour's parables related to the King's wedding feast, when invitations were despatched to many citizens. The royal host said, " Come, for the wedding is ready . . . *and they would not come.*" Together, these Scriptures provide a striking sequence of thought.

God said, " Come," and they would not come

The prophet Isaiah stood beside the bedside of his king; he was very sad. The solemnity of that occasion greatly impressed his soul, for in later days he wrote, " In the year that King Uzziah died I saw also the Lord. . . . Also I heard the voice of the Lord, saying, Whom shall I send, and who will go for us? Then said I, Here am I; send me. And he said, Go. . . ." (Isa. 6:1-8). Commissioned by God, the young man went forth to preach, and a study of his writings reveals three things. (i) *A great desire*. God longed to meet the need of His people; to pardon their sins; to place peace within their hearts. The first message to be proclaimed said, " Come now, and let us reason together, said the Lord; though your sins be as scarlet, they shall be as white as snow. . . ." (1:18). (ii) *A great decision*. " In returning and rest shall ye be saved; in quietness and in confidence shall be your strength: *and ye would not.*" The people preferred their own ideas; they liked to indulge in sin. (iii) *A great disaster*. The Lord gave to them the bread of adversity and the water of affliction. It is true that ultimately the nation was restored to Palestine; but before this was accomplished, many graves were left in Babylon.

Christ said, " Come," and they would not come

The Saviour was strangely moved as He looked at the city of God. A cross loomed upon the horizon, and soon the little sepulchre in Joseph's garden would be occupied. Jesus had come to look for the last time upon the city He loved, and His lament that day revealed the same thoughts expressed in Isaiah's ministry. (i) *A great desire.* " O Jerusalem, Jerusalem . . . how often would I have gathered thy children together, even as a hen gathereth her chickens under her wings. . . ." (ii) *A great decision.* ". . . and ye would not." There were times when even Christ was powerless. There were situations which defied even His capabilities. Christ called to, but never compelled men to trust him. (iii) *A great disaster.* " Behold, your house is left unto you desolate." When Christ turned away from the city He was indescribably sad. He knew that Roman legions would utterly devastate the place; the streets would run with blood, and He was unable to prevent the catastrophe. He realised that in the distant future the nation would exclaim, " Blessed is he that cometh in the name of the Lord ": but in the meanwhile, many graves would appear in Israel.

The king said " Come," and they would not come

The palace was filled with excitement; the wedding of the prince was at hand. " And the king sent forth his servants to call them that were bidden to the wedding: *and they would not come.* Again he sent forth other servants. . . . But they made light of it. . . ." The Lord Jesus excelled in the art of painting word-pictures, and His hearers were very attentive when He continued, " But when the king heard thereof, he was wroth: and he sent forth his armies, and destroyed them . . . and burnt up their homes." (i) *A great desire.* God is to honour His Son; it is planned that the Marriage Supper of the Lamb shall be the greatest event in history. The news of the event has been broadcast throughout the earth, but both Jews and Gentiles are reluctant to accept the invitation to the wedding. (ii) *A great decision.* This Scripture provides an eloquent commentary on the attitude of sinful people. The ancients were concerned only with material prosperity; they were dressed in modern garb! (iii) *A great disaster.* It is appointed unto men once to die, and after death the judgment. " What shall it profit a man if he gain the whole world and lose his soul? " The Bible indeed is one book; it has *one message.* Wise men will remember that this message declares, " There is a way that seemeth right unto a man, but the end thereof are the ways of death " (Prov. 14:12).

> Come to the Saviour now,
>   He gently calleth thee;
> In true repentance bow,
>   Before Him bend the knee:

He waiteth to bestow
　　Salvation, peace, and love,
True joy on earth below,
　　A home in heaven above:
　　　Come, come, come!

Bishop Taylor Smith's Barber

The late Bishop Taylor Smith was one of the most acceptable British preachers during the first half of the twentieth
century. His attractive personality, his scintillating humour,
his thought-provoking message appealed to innumerable
people, and wherever he ministered great crowds listened
attentively. Some of his illustrations were exceptionally
good. Not the least of these was his account of the London
barber who had certain things to say to his celebrated client.
Recognising that a bishop was sitting in the chair, the barber
decided to engage the customer in a religious conversation.
He said, " Do you believe in consecration, sir? "

" Consecration," replied the bishop, " what do you mean? "

The questioner seemed a little nonplussed, and could only
answer, " You ought to know what I mean, sir. I was consecrated myself once, but it never did me any good. I never
got anything out of it."

The bishop smiled and said, " I think you mean you were
confirmed."

The barber apologised, confessing that he had become a
little mixed up in his terminology. The bishop soon put the
man at ease, and added, " Tell me about your confirmation."

The barber explained that during his school days certain
children were to be confirmed, and to make this possible were
to be awarded a half-holiday. This reward seemed most attractive, and to gain a brief respite from school, he and his
friend decided to be confirmed. " So we were confirmed, sir;
but we never got anything out of it."

The bishop asked, " And did you get your half-holiday? "
" Yes, sir."

Taylor Smith laughed when he replied, " Don't say you
never got anything out of it, for you did."

The barber hastened to add, " But, sir, I didn't get what
was to be expected. Getting confirmed did not do me any
good." The tradesman was puzzled when the bishop asked,
" What did you expect to get out of your confirmation? "
When there was no reply, Bishop Taylor Smith continued,
" Confirmation means strengthening. But it is not possible
to strengthen that which does not even exist. If a man does
not possess Christian faith, it can hardly be strengthened."
Then the bishop asked a rather pointed question, " Barber,
are you going to heaven? "

" Going to heaven. Why, of course I am going to heaven. Why shouldn't I? "

The bishop replied, " But why should you? "

" Well, I'm as good as any other man. I'm always doing my best. I never do any harm to people."

The bishop said, " Is that all? Well, I'm afraid you haven't a dog's chance of getting to heaven. Barber, supposing a man came in and sat in the chair next to mine. Supposing he asked for a haircut, and I took the scissors and started on the job. What would happen? "

" Probably, sir, you would make an awful mess of it."

" Yes," responded the bishop, " but I would be doing my best." The barber sensing the direction in which the conversation was going, added, " But, sir, the more you did, the worse it would become."

" Exactly," said the bishop. " I know nothing about the art of cutting hair. But let us assume for a moment that in some strange fashion you could impart your knowledge to me; that you could control my fingers. What then? "

" Then, sir, you could cut his hair as well as I could do the job myself."

Then the bishop explained, " Barber, our best is insufficient; often, the more we try, the more we fail. Instead of relying upon our best endeavours, we yield our lives to Christ, that His Spirit can control us. Then He takes our hands with which to work; our eyes, with which to see; our lips, with which to speak; our minds, with which to think. That is the Christian life: to have Christ living in us." Soon the bishop and the barber were kneeling together, and in the years that followed, many people knew that the barber whose shop was so near to Victoria Station, London, was a true Christian. He became known as " The Consecrated Barber."

Our Mr. Schmidt

I was told the following story by a printer in the office of the Sun Publishing Company, Edmonton, Alberta, Canada. When a valuable printing press broke down, a cable summoned help from the manufacturers in Germany. In due course a young man arrived to repair the machine; but alas, the directors of the firm refused to allow the apparently inexperienced lad to touch the expensive machinery. They sent another cable to Germany, asking for a competent mechanic. The manufacturers replied, " Please allow our Mr. Schmidt to handle the machine. He made it; he should be able to repair it."

BELSHAZZAR . . . who knocked down all the fences

The late P.C. Dawes was once on point duty in Oxford-street, London, when a boat-race fan flippantly asked, "I say, Bobbie, can you tell me the way to hell? " The policeman answered immediately, " Certainly, sir. Keep straight on." There are people who believe that the way to disaster is the easiest road in life—a man merely keeps straight on, and without any difficulty reaches his disastrous end. That is not true. God never ceases to seek a man until the sinner is beyond redemption. The road to hell is filled with barriers —all erected by the love of God; and if a man is ultimately lost, it can only be because he has resisted every attempt to turn him from his way of evil. The story of Belshazzar provides a classic example of this truth.

The Testimony of a Transformed Father

The conversion of Nebuchadnezzar provides one of the most thrilling accounts in Old Testament literature. An arrogant, unbelieving pagan had been reduced to a position of mental impotence; but when hope of his recovery had been abandoned, a miracle took place. Later, the restored monarch was able to say, " And at the end of the days, I Nebuchadnezzar lifted up mine eyes unto heaven, and mine understanding returned unto me, and I blessed the most High " (Dan. 4:34). Returning to his palace, the converted king turned his home into a cathedral, and the charm of his testimony reached everybody. Yet the prince, deprived of power by the return of his father, scowled. Thus did he sweep from his path the first fence which God had placed before him. His father's testimony *might* have led him to happiness.

The Influence of a Noble Lady

This noble Babylonian queen was one of the lesser-known characters of the Scriptures, but she was a great soul. Knowing that her husband's party had become a place of fear, she said, ". . . let not thy thoughts trouble thee, nor let thy countenance be changed: There is a man in thy kingdom in whom is the spirit of the holy gods, and in the days of thy father light and understanding and wisdom, like the wisdom of the gods, was found in him. . . ." (5:10-11). Obviously, she had been attentive to Daniel's message when her foolish husband had remained indifferent; she had remembered when he had forgotten. Had that husband been more influenced by his

77

gracious lady, he might have lived longer than he did. Her presence represented God's second fence. Alas, Belshazzar swept it from his pathway.

The Ministry of a Saintly Prophet

That the boastful, evil king had ignored the preaching of the saintly Daniel did not provide him with any excuse. God may provide the preacher, but He never removes the wax from people's ears! If a man prefers to remain deaf, there is little God can do in the matter. All Babylon knew of the great Hebrew prophet, and many admired and respected him. Raised to eminence by Nebuchadnezzar, Daniel had more than justified the confidence placed in him. The prophet represented God's intervention in the affairs of men. Through him came the word of the Highest; yet in foolish arrogance the new king treated this third obstacle as he had treated the first two. Surely his sinful folly surpassed anything previously known in the country.

The Promptings of a Troubled Conscience

The palace was a scene of resplendent gaiety; the hanging gardens of Babylon were a paradise. From near and far the guests had assembled for the magnificent occasion, and the fact that enemies were encamped at the city gates meant nothing. The high encircling walls of Babylon were insurmountable; the city itself was thought to be impregnable. The wine was flowing freely; the laughter of drunken guests echoed through the night. Then, " Belshazzar, while he tasted the wine, commanded to bring the golden and silver vessels which his father Nebuchadnezzar had taken out of the temple which was in Jerusalem." How strange that in the midst of such gaiety the king should suddenly think of God. Surely this was an uprising of conscience? We can only speculate as to the length of time which elapsed before his violent reactions began. Stupid man! God had erected the last fence on the road to the eternal shadows. Belshazzar's stupidity ruthlessly trampled the obstacles beneath his feet when he sent for the consecrated vessels and continued his blasphemy. And " In the same hour came forth fingers of a man's hand, and wrote . . . on the wall of the king's palace. . . . Thou art weighed in the balances and found wanting." Yet no man is finally rejected until love has done everything possible to save him. God only abandons a man when nothing else remains to be done.

The Red Lights of Danger

The Second World War revealed many tragedies, but none more poignant than the sorrow which overwhelmed one of

Britain's greatest families. England was extremely fortunate in possessing great leaders, and among those who assisted Sir Winston Churchill was a man of outstanding ability. His sterling character, unceasing devotion to duty, and exemplary conduct, were qualities which begat confidence. Yet that same eminent man, had he desired, could have listened nightly to his own son broadcasting lies on behalf of a brutal enemy. Probably the son's betrayal of his country only increased the determination of the father to be one of England's most dependable statesmen. Throughout the long and bitter conflict he enjoyed the confidence of the people he represented. If his foolish boy had listened to the wise counsel of his illustrious father, the son's fate would have been less ignominious. When the war ended the traitor was captured, tried, and executed; but all England mourned—not for the son, but for the family whose hearts had been broken.

I shall always remember the lady in Wales who asked if I would be kind enough to take her husband to see a specialist. For many years he had suffered from a chronic complaint, but now it was hoped the famous doctor might be able to suggest an effective remedy. I did as I was requested, and finally accompanied the sufferer into the consulting room of the eminent physician. The place was filled with instruments the like of which I had never seen. The doctor was obviously a man of great capability, and for him at least, time did not even exist. With care and deliberation he examined my friend; he fastened instruments to the arms and legs of the patient, and took readings on various machines. He seemed determined to solve the problem. Finally he replaced his instruments, and cheered us all by saying, "Yes, I can cure you; but you must obey my instructions. You must never smoke again." I recalled how the patient had been a very heavy smoker for many years, and wondered what reactions would follow the giving of this advice. When the doctor's fee had been paid we returned to my car, and within thirty seconds my friend said, " Bust him; what does he know about it? " Then he proceeded to light a cigarette. Not long afterward, I attended his funeral.

The storm was at its height, and the harbour at Wick, Caithness, had been closed for hours. Very heavy seas had been pounding the breakwater, and the barometer was still falling. Outside, a few vessels were riding out the storm; but suddenly a Dutch vessel began to approach the harbour entrance. The captain was told to stay outside, but disobeying the order and ignoring the warning red lights, brought his vessel through the entrance. The many onlookers were horrified as the ship was swept round the harbour and overturned, with the loss of all hands. The skipper had a date with a Scottish girl, and was anxious to keep his appointment. The prospect of a night's pleasure cost him his life. There are times when God places warning signals within the human conscience. Happy is that soul who reads the signs and stays in safety.

I knew a man who often passed my church, yet never attended any meeting. He was brutal in his criticism, and professed to be something of an atheist. Most of his free time was spent in the hotel, and most of his money left with the bar-keeper. He was a well-known character, but every attempt to reach his soul with the Gospel seemed doomed to failure. It was 1.30 a.m., when a knock at my door announced a caller. Mr. —— was dying. Would I please come at once? I had been ill for days, but responded to the call and went to see the sick man. Yet even as I walked down the street, I wondered why the relatives had not sent for the manager of the hotel—he knew him far more intimately than I did. When I reached the house the man was unconscious, and although I sat, and hoped, and prayed, for a long time, he never regained consciousness. That was the moment of most awful frustration I ever knew. A very needy soul lay within feet of me, yet was beyond my reach! The family had sent for me too late. I had been in the town for eight years, but had never been able to enter that home. Probably Daniel would have appreciated my feelings of frustration. He had ministered in his city for years, but the king never became interested until his opportunities had gone for ever.

"Now is the accepted time; now is the day of salvation." "Come now, and let us reason together, saith the Lord: though your sins be as scarlet, they shall be as white as snow; though they be red like crimson, they shall be as wool" (Isa. 1 : 18).

How can I say "Tomorrow," when the Saviour says "Today ?"

DANIEL . . . who opened his windows

(DANIEL 6:10)

The dawn was breaking over old Babylon; the city would soon be awake. Probably the breeze was beginning to stir the flowers in the ornate hanging gardens, as the rising sun shed radiance over the ancient streets. And at his window stood Daniel the Hebrew. His eyes were those of a seer; his face was that of a saint. It would be interesting to know when he first decided to open his windows toward Jerusalem. His act was not the commonplace deed of an ordinary citizen, but the planned intelligent act of a visionary. Through his windows many worlds may still be seen.

Daniel . . . who opened his Bible

We may never be sure whether Daniel was taught by the elders, or whether he discovered truth for himself. When the Hebrews were carried into captivity, they either took the sacred writings in their luggage or the message in their hearts, for long afterward in the city of Babylon, they were able to recall the words from 1 Kings 8:45-49. "Then hear thou in heaven their prayer and their supplication, and maintain their cause . . . if they shall bethink themselves in the land *whither they were carried captives,* and repent . . . *and pray unto Thee toward their land* . . . Then hear thou their prayer. . . ." Long and often Daniel looked at the immortal statement, and then with calm deliberation rose to open his windows. His actions were magnificently eloquent.

Daniel . . . who opened his soul

"Yet if they . . . repent and make supplication unto thee in the land of them that carried them away captives, saying, *We have sinned, and have done perversely, we have committed wickedness;* and so return unto thee with all their heart, and with all their soul in the land of their enemies . . . and pray toward their land . . . then hear thou their prayer. . . ." Through the window in Babylon Daniel looked toward Jerusalem; through that same window we may look into the Hebrew's soul. Remembering the words of Solomon, Daniel's act was an open confession of sin; and this is all the more thought-provoking in view of the fact that there is no record of Daniel's failure. He was probably the most saintly man in Babylon, but he himself would have strenuously denied the assertion. Great saints invariably believe they are the chief of sinners (see Dan. 9:3-19).

Daniel . . . who opened his windows

Probably Daniel, having read the ancient account, proceeded to emulate Solomon's example, for it is written, ". . . and when Solomon had made an end of praying all this prayer and supplication unto the Lord, he arose . . . from kneeling on his knees, with his hands spread up to heaven." His soul yearned for the blessing which only God could give; but conscious of his unworthiness, the saint knew how to express the deep desires of his heart. Undoubtedly he confessed his guilt, his need, and his faith; and when in due course he arose to meet the demands of a new day, like Solomon of old, he could have cried, " Blessed be the Lord. . . ." Here is progression of thought. The Holy Scriptures are a searchlight revealing both the need of man and the sufficiency of God. Daniel would have appreciated the chorus—

> Make the Book live to me, O Lord;
> Show me myself within Thy word:
> Show me myself and show me my Saviour,
> And make the Book live to me.

Daniel . . . who opened the heavens

There is a basic law in Scripture which provides the key to spiritual prosperity. God has said, ". . . prove me . . . if *I will not open the windows of heaven,* and pour you out a blessing, that there shall not be room enough to receive it. And I will rebuke the devourer for your sakes " (Mal. 3:10-11). If we open our windows toward God, He opens His windows toward us. This was proved by the prophet Daniel. The Hebrew was penitent, prayerful, powerful; and the devourers were indeed rebuked, for the ancient records say, " And the king commanded, and they brought those men which had accused Daniel, and they cast them into the den of lions. . . ." God's word says, " I will honour them who honour me."

Daniel . . . who opened the future

" And the Lord said . . . I am come to make thee understand what shall befall thy people in the latter days " (Dan. 10:14). Daniel became God's instrument to instruct the world, and as a reward for faithful service was given a priceless promise. " But go thou thy way till the end be: for thou shalt rest, and stand in thy lot at the end of the days " (12:13). This man was the greatest window-opener of all time; but there is reason to believe he opened more windows when he was on his knees than he ever did when he was on his feet!

Are your windows open toward Jerusalem
    Whilst as captives here a little while you stay?
For the coming of the King in His glory
    Are you watching day by day?

The Woman who Interceded for D. L. Moody

In his book, *Power through Prayer,* the Rev. E. M. Bounds
tells a remarkable story. I take the liberty of re-telling this,
and at the same time to commend Mr. Bounds' thrilling
book to all my readers. On page 148 he writes, " When
D. L. Moody's church in Chicago lay in ashes, he went over
to England, not to preach, but to listen to others preach,
while his new church was being built. One Sunday morning
he was prevailed upon to preach in a London pulpit. But
somehow the spiritual atmosphere was lacking. He confessed
afterward that he never had such a hard time preaching in his
life. Everything was perfectly dead, and, as he vainly tried
to preach, he said to himself, ' What a fool I was to consent
to preach. I came here to listen, and here I am preaching.'
Then the awful thought came to him that he had to preach
again that night, and only the fact that he had given the
promise to do so, kept him faithful to the engagement. But
when Mr. Moody entered the pulpit at night, and faced the
crowded congregation, he was conscious of a new atmosphere.
' The powers of an unseen world seemed to have fallen on
the audience.' As he drew toward the close of his sermon he
became emboldened to give out an invitation, and as he concluded, said, ' If there is a man or woman here who will
tonight accept Jesus Christ, please stand up.' At once about
500 people rose to their feet. Thinking that there must be
some mistake, he asked the people to be seated, and then,
in order that there could be no possible misunderstanding,
repeated the invitation, couching it in even more definite
and difficult terms. Again the same number arose. Still
thinking that something must be wrong, Mr. Moody for the
second time asked the standing men and women to be seated,
and then invited all who really meant to accept Christ to
pass into the vestry. Fully five hundred people did as
requested, and that was the beginning of a revival in that
church and neighbourhood. This brought Mr. Moody back
from Dublin, a few days later, that he might assist the wonderful work of God.

" The sequel, however, must be given, or our purpose in
relating the incident will be defeated. When Mr. Moody
preached at the morning service, there was a woman in the
congregation who had an invalid sister. When she returned
home she told the invalid that the preacher had been a Mr.
Moody from Chicago, and on hearing this, the sister turned

pale. 'What,' she said, 'Mr. Moody from Chicago! I read about him some time ago in an American paper, and I have been praying God to send him to our country and our church. If I had known he was going to preach this morning I would have eaten no breakfast. Now, sister, go out of the room, lock the door, send me no dinner; no matter who comes, don't let them see me. I am going to spend the whole afternoon and evening in prayer.' And so while Mr. Moody stood in the pulpit that had been like an ice-chamber in the morning, the bed-ridden saint was holding him up before God. The Lord, Who ever delights to answer prayer, poured out His Spirit in mighty power."

" Mr. Hyde, Please Pray for Me "

One of the outstanding prayer warriors of this country was Praying Hyde. The story of his life and spiritual exploits has often been told, so that today even the youngest Christians know something of this great saint. During the year 1911, Mr. Hyde attended a mission service where Dr. Wilbur Chapman and Charles Alexander were having a very difficult time. Appreciating the difficulties confronting the evangelists, Mr. Hyde decided to pray the mission through to victory. When his prayers had been fully answered, and the power of God was falling continually upon the gatherings, Dr. Chapman, recognising the spiritual greatness of his friend, asked Mr. Hyde to pray for him. Some time later the renowned preacher wrote of the memorable experience when his desire was granted.

" He came to my room, turned the key in the door, dropped on his knees, waited five minutes without a single syllable coming from his lips. I could hear my own heart thumping and beating. I felt the hot tears running down my face. I knew I was with God. . . . Then with upturned face down which the tears were running, he said, ' Oh God! ' Then for five minutes at least he was still again, and then, when he knew he was talking with God, his arm went around my shoulder, and there came up from the depth of his heart such petitions for men as I had never heard before. I rose from my knees to know what real prayer was. We believe that prayer is mighty, and we believe it as we never did before."

> Prayer is the soul's sincere desire,
>   Uttered, or unexpressed:
> The motion of a hidden fire
>   That trembles in the breast.

DANIEL ... who refused to close his windows

The Babylonian presidents and princes were leaving the royal palace; they were jubilant. Their leader held a document which would mean the realisation of all their dreams. The upstart Daniel would soon be in his place! They were convinced of three things: (i) *The king would not break his word.* He had signed the decree which could mean the death of Daniel. (ii) *Daniel would never betray his faith.* Not even the threat of martyrdom would change his daily routine of worship. (iii) *Their plan was flawless.* The Hebrew would soon be thrown to the lions; their path to pre-eminence would no longer be blocked by a foreigner. Poor Daniel!

How Great His Wisdom

" Now when Daniel knew that the decree was signed, he went into his house . . . *and prayed.*" He refused to panic. It would appear from earlier chapters that this home had often been a place of refuge. Daniel had turned his home into a sanctuary. When problems harassed his soul, when danger threatened, Daniel invariably " went into his house " (see 2:17). This man could have protested to the king, or he might have tried to gain sympathy from his friends in the kingdom. The wise Hebrew never did anything until he had first drawn near to God.

How Great His Courage

" He went into his house, and *his windows being open* . . . he prayed." Did he pause to look at the open windows? Did a sinister voice whisper, " Daniel, don't be a fool. Trouble will come soon enough without your looking for it. Close the windows, or your enemies might see you in prayer." Did he smile and recognise that even a closed window could testify? Had he succumbed to that temptation, he would have (i) ruined his testimony, (ii) troubled his mind, (iii) disappointed his God, and (iv) hindered his prayer. No, the window should stay open. It would be better to die in the sunshine than live in the shadows.

How Great His Faith

". . . his windows being open . . . *toward Jerusalem.*" Possibly Daniel had other windows in his house, for he had attained to a degree of eminence within the Babylonian court. His windows were not open merely to permit the entry of fresh air! Beyond the distant horizons lay the city of his fathers, the city of his God. Faith burned as a light within his soul. The God of Abraham, Isaac, and Jacob was his God; the old city was his real home, and some day his faith would be vindicated. The nation would go back to Jerusalem.

How Great His Humility

". . . he went into his house . . . and *kneeled upon his knees.*" Daniel never knelt before any other. This man often entered into the presence of the king; this counsellor often held audience with the greatest of earth's dignitaries; but he knelt only when he came before God. Greatness was born on his knees! He succeeded in reaching the stars when he prostrated himself before the Almighty. Other men, filled with pride, would have boasted of their magnificence; but Daniel constantly stayed at the feet of his God. His strength lay in his consecration.

How Great His Persistence

". . . he kneeled upon his knees *three times a day,* and prayed. . . ." Daniel was a giant in prayer. He was never content to place a matter before God and then to sit back waiting for an answer. He besieged the throne of heaven, and persisted in his efforts until something happened. This was not a passing phase in his life; it was the habit of a life-time, and undoubtedly accounted for his mighty triumphs. Daniel 10:1-13 reveals that on one occasion he prayed for three weeks; and probably had the answer been further delayed, he would have prayed for three months. He believed in both God and his cause. He could see no reason why God should *not* intervene, and therefore he continued praying until God did something. This is true prayer.

How Great His Gratitude

". . . he prayed and *gave thanks* before his God, as he did aforetime." It is worthy of note that he did not only pray: he *gave thanks.* It is easy to give thanks when God has already done something. It is not quite as simple to do that *before* the miracle has taken place. The threat of death lay over Daniel's head. Undoubtedly he hoped that God would intervene on his behalf; but since the ways of God are sometimes unpredictable, there remained the possibility that Daniel would still be thrown to the lions. Yet he continued to give thanks. Had he the assurance that God would deliver him? ". . . he prayed and gave thanks " . . . for what? Did he praise God for (i) past mercies, (ii) present peace of mind, (iii) future deliverance? Perhaps all three were expressed in his symphony of praise. Daniel was God's man, and even the lions recognised the fact when they reclined at his feet. They felt singularly honoured that he had come to visit their home.

Hudson Taylor, whose Prayer changed the Weather

New Guinea is one of the most rugged countries in the world. High mountain ranges, intense tropical storms, and in places heavy seas crashing on sunken reefs, are sufficient to bring fear to the hearts of all travellers. Hudson Taylor, the famous missionary, had cause to know this, when on his way to China in 1853. Usually a breeze would spring up after sunset, and continue through the night until dawn. It was customary to make the maximum use of this, for during the calm daylight hours there was danger of drifting on to the reefs. Hudson Taylor described what took place.

"We were in dangerous proximity to the north of New Guinea. Saturday night had brought us to a point some thirty miles off the land, and during the Sunday morning service, which was held on deck, I could not fail to see that the captain looked troubled and frequently went over to the side of the ship. When the service was ended I learned from him the cause. A four-knot current was carrying us toward some sunken reefs, and we were already so near that it seemed improbable that we could get through the afternoon in safety. After dinner, the longboat was put out and all hands endeavoured, without success, to turn the ship's head from the shore. After standing together on the deck for some time in silence, the captain said to me, 'Well, we have done everything that can be done. We can only await the result.' A thought occurred to me, and I replied, 'No, there is one thing we have not done yet.' 'What is that?' he queried. 'Four of us on board are Christians. Let us each retire to his own cabin, and in agreed prayer ask the Lord to give us immediately a breeze. He can as easily send it now as at sunset.' The captain complied with this proposal . . . I had a good but brief season in prayer, and then felt so satisfied that our request was granted that I could not continue asking, and very soon went up again on deck. The first officer, a godless man, was in charge. I went over and asked him to let down the corners of the mainsail. . . . 'What would be the good of that?' he asked roughly. I told him we had been asking a wind from God, and that it was coming immediately; and we were so near the reef by this time that there was not a minute to lose. With an oath and a look of contempt, he said he would rather see a wind than hear of it. But while he was speaking I watched his eye, following it up to the royal; and there, sure enough, the corner of the topmost sail was beginning to tremble in the breeze. 'Don't you see the wind is coming? Look at the royal,' I exclaimed. 'No, it's only a cat's paw (a mere puff of wind). 'Cat's paw or not,' I cried, ' please let down the mainsail and give us the benefit.' This he was not slow to do. In another minute the heavy tread of the men on deck brought up the captain from his cabin to see what was the matter. The breeze had indeed come. In a few minutes we were ploughing our way at six or seven knots an hour through the water . . . and though the wind was sometimes unsteady, we did not altogether lose it until after passing the Pelew Islands. . . . Thus God encouraged me ere landing on China's shores to bring every variety of need to Him in prayer, and to expect that He would honour the name of the Lord Jesus and give the help each emergency required."

The Pilot's Face

Robert Louis Stevenson once told of a fearful storm at sea when a vessel seemed in imminent danger of sinking. As the waves repeatedly broke over the decks, the passengers were very frightened; but one of them, disobeying orders, went on deck, to see the pilot lashed to the wheel. Calmly the man was getting on with his task, and suddenly seeing the terror-stricken passenger, the pilot gave him a reassuring smile. Instantly a change came over the fearful traveller, and when he rejoined the others below deck, he said, " I have seen the face of the pilot, and he smiled. All is well." Surely that pilot would have appreciated Daniel's faith. Throughout the city of Babylon, storms were threatening to bring disaster to the people of God. Daniel was in great danger, yet he smiled. He had seen the face of God; he knew all would be well.

I once looked through the window of my church to see a small boy, Brinley Howells, banging on the front door knocker of his home. What I saw fascinated me, for the lad was using one hand to continue knocking while his other hand held up the flap of the letter-box. He knew his mother would respond to his call, and was actually looking through the opening to see her coming. In some senses that, even now, seems to be my most vivid illustration of believing prayer. It is insufficient merely to ask God to come; we should be looking for His appearance even while we ask.

CHRIST . . . Who refused to take a short cut

(MATTHEW 4:8-10)

The Lord Jesus Christ came into this world with a passion to win the lost. He had no illusions as to what this might mean, and even from the beginning contemplated His crucifixion. Yet in one sinister moment, Satan unfolded a plan to solve all the problems of evangelism. " Again, the devil . . . sheweth him all the kingdoms of the world, and the glory of them; and saith unto him, All these things will I give thee, if thou wilt fall down and worship me." In those vital moments the world seem to be spread as a map at the feet of the Saviour. He saw India, China, and Japan. He saw the jungle villages of central Africa; He saw the crowded cities of Western civilisation; He saw the lonely islands of the sea, and realised that in all these places Satan would resist the eternal purposes of God. Bitter would be the conflict, long would be the campaign before the world could be won; and even then the victory would hardly be complete, for many souls would have passed into eternity. Against this background, Satan made his insidious offer.

Purity . . . the foundation of all true usefulness

We do well to consider that Christ never challenged Satan's ability to do as was suggested. The record given by Luke is even more pointed: " And the devil said unto him, All this power will I give thee, and the glory of them, for that is delivered unto me; and to whomsoever I will give it. If thou therefore wilt worship me, all shall be thine " (4:6, 7). The temptation suggests that Satan offered to withdraw all his opposition. There would be no more surging passions; no more vice, wickedness, godlessness. The heart of Africa would be open and free from superstition; the underworld of the great cities would become clean overnight; and the entire world would be released from the thraldom of sin and brought back to God. " All this will I give thee, if ——." From every human angle, the offer was most attractive; but the Lord Jesus refused. It therefore became clear that He considered the integrity of His own soul to be of more importance than the winning of the world. The end never justifies the means if the means destroy the sanctity of the soul. The evil one offers many attractive rewards, but his conditional *if* is always the prelude to disaster.

Preaching . . . the forerunner of all true blessedness

After His triumph, " Jesus returned in the power of the Spirit into Galilee " (Luke 4:14). " And from that time began to preach and to say, Repent . . ." (Matt. 4:17). There can never be any substitute for preaching delivered in the power of the Holy Spirit. When the Church loses this dynamic; when the services become glorified entertainments; when the message is subservient to all the other details introduced to captivate the superficial section of the congregation, the Church is on the high road to suicide. " And Jesus, walking by the sea of Galilee . . . called Peter and Andrew . . . and he saith unto them, Follow me, and I will make you fishers of men " (vv. 18-19). These men were only converts themselves, and yet already before them was the prospect of catching men as they had often caught fish. The Lord Jesus meant to train these converts so that as quickly as possible they too could go in search of kindred souls. Evangelism has been the greatest striking force in the history of the Church. A church without a pulpit becomes a hall!

Power . . . the feature of all true godliness

" And Jesus went about all Galilee, teaching in their synagogues, and preaching the gospel of the kingdom, and healing all manner of sickness, and all manner of disease among the people. And his fame went throughout all Syria: and they brought unto him all sick people that were taken with divers diseases and torments, and those which were possessed with devils, and those which were lunatic, and those that had the palsy; and he healed them " (vv. 23, 24). And against all these remarkable statements, we must consider another promise. "And greater things than these shall ye do, because I go unto my Father " (John 14:12). It would seem that something has gone wrong with the Church. We may talk about opening the eyes of blind unbelief, of cleansing the moral leprosy from our great cities; but are these the final word in the fulfilment of Christ's promise? The power of the Church could be increased immeasurably if we resisted every attempt of Satan to impair the sanctity of our souls. Preaching is a great weapon; holiness is also a great weapon: But when these two are combined and used in the power of the divine Spirit, even the gates of hell cannot prevail against us.

The Most Beautiful Hands in the World

Dr. Don E. Falkenberg's sermon, *The Wounds of Christ,* must rank as one of the greatest utterances I have ever heard. Inspired by a medical doctor's observation, he gave close attention to the subject, and ascertained that " not only does the New Testament record the suffering of all types of flesh wounds by our Lord, but also that the Old Testament foretold each of these types." During his wonderful discourse he referred to Isaiah's writings: " And when we shall see him, there is no beauty that we should desire him. . . . We hid as it were our faces from him. . . . His visage was so marred more than any man, and his form more than the sons of man " (Isa. 53, and 52:14). Then to illustrate this poignant truth, Dr. Falkenberg told a moving story.

" In an American town resided a widowed mother and her little son. The mother was very beautiful except for her hands, which were terribly scarred as from scalding or burning. As the little lad reached the age when he began to notice the contrast between individuals, he asked his mother, ' Mumsy, why are your hands so scarred? Why aren't they beautiful like Bobby's mother's hands?' When the mother felt the lad was old enough to understand, she answered his oft-repeated question. ' When you were very small, Billy, you were playing in the living room one day, and I was working in the kitchen. Suddenly I heard you scream, and I rushed in and found you had gotten too close to the fireplace, and your clothes had caught on fire. I tore your burning clothes from your body before you were seriously burned, but my hands were deeply burned by the searing flames. That is why, Billy, I have such unlovely hands. That is why they are not beautiful.' Billy looked at those scarred hands for a moment, and then one little arm went round his mother's neck, and the other childish hand lifted one of her scarred hands to his lips for a kiss of tenderness, as he cried out in compassionate love, ' Mother, your hands aren't ugly; you have the most beautiful hands in all the world.' " Dr. Falkenberg adds, " In Christ's terribly marred face we find beauty as we realise He was wounded for our transgressions . . . with His stripes we are healed."

Working like Billiho

The story of the Rev. E. Billiho provides a graphic illustration of the wisdom of avoiding short-cuts. Billiho, so we have been told, was a minister of the Established Church during that sombre period of British history when the shackles of a crippling tradition were hindering the march of progress. Unfortunately for his family, Billiho could not accept certain doctrines and practices of the Church, and soon his voice was raised against them. The ecclesiastical leaders becoming alarmed, threatened to deprive this renegade of his living; he was told to restrain his tongue, or suffer the consequences. This he could not do, and the day arrived when Billiho was defrocked and left without means to sustain his large family. His friends wondered what he would do, but were not left in doubt for very long. Billiho, with his own hands, set about the task of erecting his own church; and his ceaseless labours amazed even his closest friends. Many considered him to be foolish, for had he curbed his tongue, had he taken a short cut, he might have influenced his parishioners to accept quietly the things he believed. Billiho preferred to go the long way around, and within a short time became known as the man who never ceased labouring. Soon his new church was open, and the power of his ministry reached far and wide over the countryside of Britain. Few people seem to know that he bequeathed to posterity and the English language the household saying, "We must work like Billiho."

The hymn, *Come, Thou fount of every blessing,* was written by the Rev. R. Robinson, who was born in 1735. At the age of fourteen he was sent to London to learn the trade of hair dressing. When he became a Christian he commenced to study for the ministry, and eventually became well known as a hymn-writer. As he grew old, however, he began to lose his grasp of spiritual things, and to indulge in habits which did not adorn the Gospel. Years later, while travelling on a stage coach, he was engaged in conversation by a lady who, not knowing his identity, told him how she had been reading Robinson's hymn, *Come, Thou fount of every blessing,* and asked his opinion of its worth. The author endeavoured in vain to change the topic of conversation, but finally, unable to control his emotion, cried out, "Madam, I am the poor, unhappy man who composed that hymn many years ago. I would give a thousand worlds, if I had them, to enjoy the feelings I had then." He had sold his birthright for a mess of pottage.

THE LAST GREAT ASSIZE . . . and the witnesses for the prosecution

(MAT. 12, 41:42; MARK 6, II)

In the year A.D. 79 Vesuvius erupted, to bury the city of Pompei beneath a sea of lava and ashes. Slaves chained to their posts perished; the people who fled into their homes were suffocated; in a few hours, a city disappeared. For some inscrutable reason Pompei was forgotten, until centuries later certain monuments attracted the archaeologists, and the uncovering of the ruins commenced. In June, 1957, I walked through this scene of devastation, asking why God permitted the catastrophe. Then the guide, accompanied only by men, went into the ancient house of Vetii, and my question was answered. The eruption of Vesuvius destroyed a city of lust. The Bible declared that God will judge the world in righteousness; and when we consider the various statements of the Lord Jesus, it is possible to trace the trend of events as they are to be revealed at the final great assize.

Call the Men of Nineveh—Matthew 12:41

Let us consider that judgment day; let us see the opening of the books, and watch as the accused are brought to trial. Then, " The men of Nineveh shall rise in the judgment with this generation, and shall condemn it: because they repented at the preaching of Jonas; and behold, a greater than Jonas is here." Perhaps on God's eternal television screen will be flashed the ancient scene. We may see Jonah standing close to the sea; we may see the great mammal gently rolling in the shallow waters, while nearby the onlookers marvel at the phenomenon which had brought Jonah from his watery grave. The fish-god was dead; the preacher had returned from another world; his message was a supernatural warning —" and they repented at the preaching of Jonas." The ministry of the Lord Jesus Christ, His resurrection from the dead, the reiteration of His warning through the ages, will all unite in the condemnation of this unrepentant generation. And when the accused ask, " But how were we to know whether the message was authentic? " the recording angel will summon the next witness.

Call the Queen of Sheba—Matthew 12:42

If the ancient scene is recaptured in all its scintillating brilliance, we shall see a sight probably unsurpassed in ancient history. We shall consider again how the news of

Solomon's magnificence was carried by merchants to distant lands, and how the Queen of Sheba heard the story, and smiled. Such fantasy was surely the product of overwrought minds; the effervescence of vivid imagination. Yet the accounts continued to be told, and unable to silence her doubts, " she came from the uttermost parts of the earth to hear the wisdom of Solomon." " Queen of Sheba! Was it not beneath your dignity to travel so far on such an errand? " and the regal lady of a bygone age gracefully bows and replies, " I had nothing to lose; I had much to gain. I discovered that the half had never been told." Continues the prosecuting counsel, " Let me ask another question: What would you think of people who heard a similar message thousands of times, of people who only had a short distance to travel, and yet they lived and died debating whether the message were true or false? " The Lord Jesus said, " The Queen of Sheba shall rise up in the judgment with this generation, and shall condemn it. . . ."

Call the People of Sodom—Mark 6:11

Sodom was the most indecent of all the ancient cities, and its evil practices led to disaster. Yet the Saviour stated that in the day of judgment Sodom would be more acceptable than some of the modern respectable cities with which our present world abounds. " Men of Sodom, why did you not heed the warning of Holy Scripture? " " We had no Scripture." " Did you not attend the evangelistic meetings? " " We never had any meetings." " Did you not go to church —to Sunday-school; did you not hear a preacher? " "We never knew any of these blessings. We never saw a Bible, we never heard a hymn, we had no Gospel, no preacher. Perhaps if we had known these wonderful things, Sodom might have been a holy city." " Men of Sodom, what would you say of people who had all these advantages—a church in every street, a Bible in every home, a preacher in every pulpit? Men of Sodom, what would you say of modern folk who only have to turn a knob on a radio panel to hear as many preachers as they desire, and yet, who remain indifferent to every warning? " " Surely, such people would be fools." And before this array of witnesses sinful man must inevitably be condemned. " It is appointed unto man once to die, and after death the judgment." To be forewarned is to be forearmed. If I must appear before God's throne, I shall need the services of a competent lawyer; and it is worthy of note that the Lord Jesus offers His services without money and without price. I should consult Him before it is too late.

The Hymn that Stopped a Bullet

In his delightful book, *Sankey's Story of Sacred Songs and Solos,* Ira D. Sankey has told a remarkable tale concerning the hymn *Jesus, Lover of my soul.* " A party of tourists formed a part of a large company gathered on the deck of an excursion steamer that was moving slowly down the Potomac one beautiful evening in the summer of 1881. A gentleman who has since gained a national reputation as an evangelist of song, had been delighting the party with the happy rendering of many delightful hymns, the last being the sweet petition so dear to every Christian, *Jesus, Lover of my soul.* The singer gave the first two verses with much feeling, and a peculiar emphasis upon the concluding lines that thrilled every heart. A hush had fallen upon the listeners that was not broken for some seconds after the musical notes had died away. Then a gentleman made his way from the outskirts of the crowd to the side of the singer, and accosted him with : ' Beg your pardon, stranger, but were you actively engaged in the late war? ' 'Yes, sir,' the man of song answered courteously, ' I fought under General Grant.' ' Well,' said the first speaker, ' I did my fighting on the other side, and think, indeed am quite sure, I was very near you one bright night, eighteen years ago this very month. It was much such a night as this. If I am not very much mistaken, you were on guard duty. We of the South had sharp business on hand, and you were one of the enemy. I crept near your post of duty, my murderous weapon in my hand; the shadows hid me. As you paced back and forth you were humming the tune of the hymn you have just sung. I raised my gun and aimed at your heart; I had been selected by my commander for the work because I was a sure shot. Then out upon the night rang the words—

> Cover my defenceless head
> With the shadow of Thy wing.

" ' Your prayer was answered. I couldn't fire after that. And there was no attack made upon your camp that night. You were the man whose life I was spared from taking.'

" The singer grasped the hand of the Southerner, and said with much emotion, ' I remember that night very well, and also the feeling of depression and loneliness with which I went forth to my duty. I knew my post was one of great danger, and I was more dejected than I remember to have been at any other time during the service. I paced my lonely beat, thinking of home and friends, and all that life holds dear. Then the thought of God's care for all that He had created came to me with peculiar force. If He so cared for the sparrows, how much more for man, created in His own image? and I sang the prayer of my heart, and ceased to be alone. How the prayer was answered I never knew till this evening.' "

Henry Ward Beecher once said of this same hymn, " I would rather have written that hymn of Wesley's, *Jesus, Lover of my soul*, than to have the fame of all the kings that ever sat on earth. It is more glorious, it has more power in it. I would rather be the author of that hymn than to hold the wealth of the richest man in New York. It will go on singing until the trump brings forth the angel band; and then I think it will mount up on some lip to the very presence of God."

" I'm Going to See the Saviour "

I knew her very, very well; I had reason for this, for mine was the privilege of leading her to Christ. She had been a great sinner, and although she never referred to her past, the shadows which periodically crossed her face suggested she could not altogether forget what had taken place. She had frequented the indecent parts of her town; she had more or less lived on the proceeds of immorality. And then she met the Saviour. I cannot recall how she first came to my services: I only know that a crusade was being held in her town, and that one night this pale young woman entered the building, found a seat, and listened attentively to my story of Jesus. She was undoubtedly troubled. Responding to the challenge, she asked the Lord for forgiveness, and from that moment demonstrated the reality of her conversion. She did not live very long, but when the end drew near some of her Christian friends endeavoured to encourage her to get well. Radiance illumined her face when she said, " But I don't want to get well. I'm going to see the Saviour, and that is all I want." Very soon her desire was granted. She left a fragrance behind; and although the years are swiftly passing, its beauty never seems to diminish. The day of judgment held no terror for her; her sins no longer tormented her conscience. She had found refuge in the Lord Jesus; within His arms she had found sanctuary.

THE STONE THROWER ... who lived in a glass house

(MATTHEW 18:23-35)

Power in the Church will never be possible unless peace reigns in the assembly. "Behold, how good and how pleasant it is for brethren to dwell together in unity . . . for there the Lord commanded the blessing, even life for evermore" (Ps. 133). Christ's memorable words had so impressed Simon Peter that the disciple said: "Lord, how oft shall my brother sin against me, and I forgive him? till seven times?" The Saviour answered, "I say not unto thee, Until seven times: but, Until seventy times seven." Probably He realised that Simon Peter would be far too impatient to continue counting—it would be infinitely easier to continue forgiving. Then followed one of the most amazing illustrations.

Grace Delivering

"Therefore is the kingdom of heaven likened unto a certain king, who would take account of his servants. And when he had begun to reckon, one was brought unto him, which owed him ten thousand talents." According to the *Standard International Encyclopedia* a talent of silver would be worth £410. A talent of gold would be worth £6,150. It is impossible to say which of these the Master had in mind, but if the servant owed that number of silver talents, then he was indebted for £4,100,000. If the talents were of gold, he owed sixty-one and a half million pounds. To say the least, that amount is staggering. Let us read the account again. "One was brought unto him, which owed him £61,500,000 (172,815,000 dollars). But forasmuch as he had nothing to pay, his lord commanded him to be sold, and his wife, and children, and all that he had, and payment to be made." The immensity of the debt suggests questions. In what way did the debt increase to such an extent? It would seem that this man held a very responsible position—a position of trust in the kingdom. Perhaps he was the Minister of Finance—the Chancellor of the Exchequer. If that were the case, his sin was even more grievous. And what had become of the money? It might be possible to account for a slight discrepancy, but it would be hard to explain the disappearance of 61 million. Someone was guilty! The man had no excuses to offer. Yet when he asked for mercy, the king's grace granted his request. "If we confess our sins, he is faithful and just to forgive us. . . ."

Guilt Demanding

"But the same servant went out and found one of his fellow servants which owed him £3 2s. 6d.—8 dollars, 50 cents —(a 'penny' is the Roman *denarius*, worth 7½d.), and he laid hands on him, and took him by the throat, saying, Pay me that thou owest. And his fellow servant fell down at his feet, and besought him, saying, Have patience with me, and I will pay thee all. *And he would not*: but went and cast him into prison, till he should pay the debt." He was a man with a poor memory! He seemed to know nothing of the great law of life—Do unto others as you would have them do to you. However, we must not forget that this story was given in reply to Peter's words about forgiving seven times. The Lord answered, "Until seventy times seven," but His illustration reveals the need for higher mathematics in reaching a complete answer. If the talent in question were a talent of gold, and if the £3 2s. 6d. had to be multiplied until both debts were almost equal, then the financier would need to forgive his fellow servant—not seventy times seven, but nearly three million times seven. This would be almost a thousand times per day every day from ten to seventy years. Such figures are apt to make us dizzy, but we must remember that thus did Christ refer to the debt of gratitude we owe to God. It matters not what we may be called upon to suffer; whatever injustices we may face. We have been forgiven far more than we shall ever be required to forgive. Therefore, bitterness should never inhabit our hearts.

Gratitude Demonstrating

"And his lord was wroth, and delivered him to the tormentors, till he should pay all that was due unto him. So likewise shall my heavenly Father do unto you, if ye from your hearts forgive not every one his brother their trespasses." These are solemn words. Will God be angry if my actions betray a lack of sympathetic understanding bordering on hypocrisy? Is it possible that some of the benefits of grace might be denied me because of my unworthiness? I do not know. This verse may contain depths of teaching hard to fathom, but the warning is clear. *People who live in glass-houses should never throw stones.* And thus did Christ reveal that unity in the Church is an essential. When people become annoyed with each other, they should meet together in the spirit of humility—forgiving one another, even as they have been forgiven, and always, "there am I in the midst of them."

In Search of Wisdom

"The story of In Ho Oh is not very long; it was cut short

when it was just getting nicely under way, but it is worth remembering and thinking about. At the time of his death, In Ho Oh was a student at the University of Pennsylvania. He had gone to the United States soon after the Korean war. In Korea he had studied theology at the Seoul National University; and his parents, who are devout Christians, thought themselves very fortunate that they could send their son to complete his studies in a Christian country. They had encouraged him to dream of going to the United States, and in his mind, America had become the Promised Land.

" When he arrived, he took up his studies at the Eastern Baptist College in Philadelphia, and then went on to the University of Pennsylvania. He did not go out often, because he was rather shy, although he had a ready smile and seemed anxious that people should like him. But one evening he went out to mail a letter home, and a group of school-age boys stopped him and beat him to death.

" That was early last month (May, 1958). Since then, Oh's parents have sent a message from Korea to the authorities in Philadelphia. In it they expressed the hope that the eleven boys accused of killing Oh will receive the '*most lenient possible treatment within the laws of your government.*' And Oh's father, who manages a textile factory in Pusan, said that he and his wife are establishing a fund which they would like to be used '*for the religious, educational, vocational and social guidance*' of the boys who killed their son.

" If In Ho Oh had lived he might have made good use of the lessons he had come so far to learn. But it is doubtful if any of those lessons could have been more profound or more difficult to grasp than the one his parents in Korea are so qualified to teach."

—*The Winnipeg Free Press, June* 3, 1958.

The Strong Silent Man

Years ago, when I was a very young preacher, I visited a certain English town in which one of the foremost Christian workers seemed a man apart. He was tall, dignified, and a little reserved. Yet a strange power emanated from his face, and although he took no public part in the various meetings, I was always conscious of his presence. My colleagues similarly became aware of his strange influence, and when we began discussing him, our leader smiled. For some time he remained thoughtful, but ultimately deciding to take us into his confidence, he told us the story of the strong, silent man.

Years earlier, when he had reached a place of importance in the community, when his life more than adorned the faith he professed, he had fallen in love with a young woman.

99

She accepted his proposal of marriage, and in due course the wedding bells rang. That same night, the first of their honeymoon, she sat on her bed and admitted she was soon to become a mother. She told of another man who had seduced and abandoned her; calmly she confessed she had entered into the marriage contract because it offered security for her unborn child. Bewildered and dismayed, her husband listened to the sordid story, and then fought the greatest battle of his career. He permitted her to stay; apparently he overlooked her glaring indiscretions, and forgot her base treachery. Only a few people ever heard the true facts, for when the child was born, the strong, silent man ignored the whispering campaign and proceeded to be a good father to his wife's child. That he had weathered the storm no one could dispute. His silent eloquence enthralled his friends. When next he came into our services I watched his kindly face, and realised more than ever how much I had to learn.

I once knew of a wagtail's nest in which a cuckoo had deposited an egg. When the young cuckoo made his appearance, he proceeded to push the other birds out of the nest. It was rather disconcerting to see this foreigner bringing disaster to the family. However, it was even more thought-provoking to watch the mother bird struggling valiantly to feed the murderer. The huge hungry baby made her appear very diminutive. He was greedy, impatient, annoying; but never for a moment did the faithful wagtail shirk her duty nor leave her task. And I wondered if my Christian principles would have been sufficiently strong to enable me to do a similar task in my particular sphere of life. To forgive and keep on forgiving; to love those who hate you; to serve those who persecute you—these are the hall-marks of greatness.

THE MASTER . . . Who knew how to preach

When the Lord Jesus instituted a new order of preaching, the reasons for His phenomenal success seemed to be three-fold. *He was sure.* He knew and believed what He uttered. *He was simple.* Even a child could understand His sermons. *He was a story-teller.* People of all ages appreciate a good story, and it is worthy of consideration that the Lord's messages were filled with parables and illustrations. The study before us supplies a notable example of this fact.

Christ . . . the final word—Mark 12:1-6

This is perhaps the most all-embracing of the Master's sermons, for in the short span of six verses He encompassed the Old Testament. (i) *God's Garden.* This must be the world into which He placed the husbandmen. Eden was but the initial stage of a greater programme. Within the orbit of the divine will, God's servants would discover superlative enjoyment. Alas, sin interfered. (ii) *Great guilt.* " And at the season God sent to the husbandmen a servant, that he might receive . . . the fruit of the vineyard. And they caught him, and beat him, and sent him away empty. And again he sent . . . another servant . . . and another; and him they killed, and many others; beating some, and killing some." This part of the parable reflected Old Testament history, where the sin of men and the patient love of God were seen in bold relief. (iii) *Glorious Grace.* " Having yet therefore *one* son, his well-beloved, he sent him also last unto them, saying, They will reverence my son." Thus God spoke His final word, and made a supreme effort to reach guilty men. This was God's *only* Son. Christ was greater than the law; Christ was greater than the prophets who spoke of the law; Christ was *the Son of God,* and no preacher can over-emphasise these claims. " God, who at sundry times and in divers places spake in times past unto the fathers by the prophets, hath in these last days spoken unto us by his Son " (Heb. 1:1-2).

Christ . . . the final hope—Mark 12:7-9

Perhaps these verses are among the most potent in the Testament. The Lord knew what would transpire, and pre-dicted some startling events. (i) *An inexcusable crime.* He knew the people would crucify Him, and He said so. Their action would not be the product of a sudden brainstorm; it would be premeditated murder. They would face the challenge of His message, and deliberately reject the Son of God. (ii) *An inescapable condemnation*. Since Christ represented God's final endeavour to reach sinners, there could be no other Saviour. When people rejected Christ, " God gave them up " (Rom. 1 : 24-26). (iii) *An indescribable calamity*. " What shall therefore the lord of the vineyard do? He will come and destroy the husbandmen . . . " There are people who dislike this teaching; but we do well to remember that these words were spoken by Christ Himself. " It is appointed unto men once to die, but after this *the judgment* (Heb. 9 : 27). Our Lord's parable speaks of the destruction of the husbandmen; and not even the most imaginative mind can read into that utterance a message of recurring hope.

Christ . . . the final triumph—Mark 12 : 10-12

" And they sought to lay hold on him . . for they knew that he had spoken this parable against them . . . " The entire story can be read aloud in seventy-five seconds, yet within that time the Lord expressed eternity. The depth of divine love, the immensity of human guilt, the reality of God's wrath: all found a place in the discourse. This was preaching at its scintillating best, but one other detail was needed to complete the picture. He continued, " And have ye not read this scripture; The stone which the builders rejected is become the head of the corner: this was the Lord's doing, and it is marvellous in our eyes?" The cross had no terrors for Christ, for He recognised it to be the highway to eternal exaltation. The rejected stone would not be permitted to stay in desolate isolation. The Supreme Architect would decree that it be reclaimed and placed in a position of magnificence—the head stone of the corner. (i) *The stone of shelter*. Most people struggling against icy winds have been glad to reach the corner of a building and walk into a place of calm. (ii) *The stone of strength*. The corner stone unites other stones in the building. The death of Christ guaranteed that there would be other stones; and these, God planned to unite in a living temple. (iii) *The stone of support*. This is particularly true of the head corner-stone, for upon it rests the roof of the building. It is a thrilling thing to know that the Lord Jesus will be our support throughout eternity. Evil may win occasional victories, but the last great triumph rests with Christ. Hallelujah!

Making Things Understood

Preaching the Gospel is a waste of time if the preacher tells his message in a way incapable of being understood by his listeners. The Saviour was a Master-preacher because everybody understood what He meant.

When a schoolboy was asked to explain the game of cricket, he said, " You have two sides, one out in the field, and one in. Each man in the side that's in goes out, and when he is out he comes in, and the next man goes in until he is out. When they are all out, the side that's been out in the field comes in, and the side that's been in goes out and tries to get those coming in out. Then when both sides have been in and out—including not outs—that's the end of the game." During the broadcast commentaries on the English Cricket Test Matches, the speakers from time to time explained the terminology of this fine old game. This became necessary because certain listeners new to the sport found it difficult to understand what was meant when the commentator frequently said, " He is bowling at the south end, and listeners will like to know that he has two fine legs, a square leg and a long leg." Newcomers to the game wondered if he were an expert talking about centipedes!

In contrast to the ambiguity of the aforegoing paragraph, the poem " He died for me," by an unknown author, seems a classic in making things clear—

> His holy fingers formed the bough
>   Where grew the thorns that crowned His brow;
> The nails which pierced His hands were mined
>   In secret places He designed.
> He made the forest whence there sprung
>   The tree on which His body hung;
> He died upon a cross of wood,
>   Yet made the hill on which it stood.
> The spear which spilt His precious blood,
>   Was tempered in the fires of God;
> The grave in which His body laid
>   Was hewn in rocks His hands had made.

Churchyards, in spite of their sombre surroundings, can be most interesting. The people of earlier generations were not as formal in their choice of epitaphs as we are, and consequently some of the older inscriptions on the tombstones are worthy of attention. For example, let me cite an instance said to come from Northern Ireland. A tramp who spent a night among the tombs was attracted to the message engraved on one of the stones—

Stop, traveller, stop! as you pass by:
As you are now, so once was I;
As I am now, so you will be:
Prepare yourself to follow me.

Possibly the tramp sheltering from the storm leaned against that stone, and had time in which to think. Before he continued his journey the following morning, he scratched beneath the strange verse the additional two lines—

To follow you I'd be quite content,
If I only knew which way you went.

"Daddy, that was the first sermon I ever understood in all my life." So spoke one of the most charming girls I ever met. She was a high-school girl in her early teens; she had passed with honours every exam, and seemed set to gain the highest academic degrees. Her father was a respected business man who had more than a love for gambling; her mother was a nominal member of the Baptist Church. I was a young preacher at that time, and conducting an evangelistic crusade in their district. Edith for the first time heard and understood the Gospel, and I was thrilled to lead her to full commitment to Christ. When she made her first confession to her father, he was stirred; but for a while disguised his true feelings. Edith's mother unashamedly confessed her delight, and re-dedicated herself to the service of her daughter's Saviour. Within a few weeks that gracious girl went home to heaven, and we were immeasurably poorer when she left us. I shall remember the day when I led her father to Christ—he was won not through my preaching, but through the glorious testimony of his beloved child. And through all the years that family has remained true to Christ. It is better to speak one sentence which is understood than to utter a thousand which only confuse listeners.

THE GREAT EVANGELIST . . . and the church He could trust

(LUKE 10:34)

The stories or parables of the Saviour were always filled with superlative interest, but few can be more intimately related to the problems of modern evangelism than the account of the Good Samaritan. How he went forth on the Jericho road, and there found an unfortunate traveller, is known to all Bible students; but strange to relate, many readers have missed a vital part of the account. When the Samaritan saw his potential convert " . . . he had compassion on him, and went to him, and bound up his wounds, pouring in oil and wine, and set him on his own beast "— and then probably asked himself a most important question, " What shall I do with him now?" " *And he brought him to an inn.*"

The Church of the Open Road

What would the Good Samaritan have done with his convert if the inn had not existed? The traveller's life was in danger; his physical condition forbade removal either to distant Jerusalem or Jericho. He needed urgent attention. Here was a problem of the first magnitude. " What can be done with my convert? Have I rescued him only to see him die in my arms?" " And he brought him to an inn . . . and said unto the host, Take care of him . . . " And there we have the crux of the problem of modern evangelism. The church has been built alongside the road of life to be a haven for travellers who need succour. Gifted evangelists may go forth seeking the lost, but without the church of the open road, much of their best efforts will be fruitless. To build an inn in such an isolated and dangerous place surely seemed ludicrous, and many readers will wonder why the innkeeper decided to embark on such a hazardous venture. That he was a man of rare vision, none will deny. Possibly he had travelled that way and had first-hand experience of the need for such accommodation. The account teaches that the ministry of the church is of equal importance with that of the man who brings the lost from the highways of life.

The Church of the Open Door

It would appear that the Good Samaritan knew the type of reception he would receive at the innkeeper's door. Here was a man whose hospitality was known far and wide. None who came were ever turned away. The innkeeper could not afford to turn people away. This was not a thriving seaside resort, nor a place of majestic scenic beauty. Wealthy citizens did not come here to retire. This inn was on the Jericho road, where robber bands terrorised travellers. If any people were refused admission there would be a possibility of the innkeeper going out of business. And in like manner, the same truth applies to the church. Without the fruits of successful evangelism, the modern church may become an eventide home for the aged. The function of the church is to keep open doors for all people—segregation is a word not found in God's dictionary. The clarion call of the church has always been, " Whosoever will may come; and him that cometh, I will in no wise cast out." Where the church has departed from this ancient standard, she has ceased to be of any spiritual value. The text, " Take care of him," should be mentioned to the assembly each time a new member is received into fellowship.

The Church of the Open Heart

The dawn was breaking; the Good Samaritan was about to leave. The innkeeper was smiling. " Friend, why not stay longer?" " Mr. Innkeeper, I cannot. Other travellers may be needing help. Yet soon I shall return. Take care of my convert, ' and whatsoever thou spendest . . . when I come again, I will repay thee.' " Thus was a man commissioned to continue the work which the Saviour had commenced. The best possible attention was lavished upon the sufferer; nothing was too much trouble, and at any time of the day or night, the kind host was ready to answer a call for assistance. The care of the convert is the duty and privilege of the church; and thus we arrive back where we started. Evangelism without the church is a flop; the church without evangelism is a social club with a religious flavour. To bring souls into the fellowship of the assembly is the prerogative of evangelism; to prepare wholesome meals enabling souls to grow into a measure of spiritual health, is the task of the church itself. The Lord gave to the church apostles, prophets, evangelists, pastors, and teachers—" for the perfecting of the saints, for the work of the ministry, for the edifying of the body of Christ " (Eph. 4:11, 12). When the evangelist and the church begin to quarrel, they both commit suicide!

The Problems and Pleasures of Church Life

We have just considered the inn on the Jericho road. We have, I trust, walked through that hospitable abode, examining every corner and interviewing the staff. Surely the home which enjoyed the confidence of the good Samaritan was a fine place indeed. Similarly, the church on the highway of life—my church, your church—should be just as wonderful. Alas, oftentimes this is not the case. Various people have said, " I can be just as good a Christian at home.. I have no need to identify myself with any church." This is not true. I have likened the church to a fire; the Christian to an individual coal. Take a tongs and separate the hottest coal from its fellows, and within seconds the living ember will begin to lose its glow. A piece of coal can only burn when it has fellowship with others. Yet the same fire which supplies great satisfaction may, out of its rightful sphere, become a source of tragic disaster. Within the church may be anything from deepest disappointment to thrilling ecstasy: it all depends—*on us*. I would like to reproduce a strange poem which I found in *The Australian Baptist*, February 12, 1958.

> Ten little churchmen went to church when fine,
> But it started raining, then there were nine;
> Nine little churchmen stayed up very late,
> One overslept himself then there were eight.
> Eight little churchmen on the road to heaven,
> One joined a rambling club, then there were seven;
> Seven little churchmen heard of Sunday " flicks,"
> One thought he'd like to go, then there were six.
> Six little churchmen kept the place alive,
> One bought a television set, and then there were five;
> Five little churchmen seemed loyal to the core,
> The pastor upset one of them, then there were four.
> Four little churchmen argued heatedly
> Over ceremonial, then there were three;
> Three little churchmen sang the service through,
> Got a hymn they didn't know, then there were two.
> Two little churchmen disputed who should run
> The next church concert, and then there was one;
> One faithful churchman, knowing what to do,
> Got a friend to come to church, then there were two.
> Two sincere churchmen each brought in one more,
> So their number doubled, then there were four;
> Four sturdy churchmen simply couldn't wait
> Till they found four others, then there were eight.
> Eight eager churchmen, searching round for souls,
> Working, praying, witnessing, drew others in by shoals;
> Shoals and shoals at every service, cramming every pew,
> O God, supply this grace and zeal in my own parish too.

Before the Good Samaritan left the inn, " he took out two pence and gave them to the host, and said unto him, Take care of him; and whatsoever thou spendest more, *when I come again*, I will repay thee." That Christ will return to meet and reward His faithful servants, is the fervent hope of the church. The following illustration from *The New Century Leader* is most suggestive.

A tourist travelling through the picturesque parts of Northern Italy came to the castle, Villa Asconati. The beautiful grounds were so well kept and attractive that he asked permission to walk through them. The gardener was delighted with the request, and gladly permitted the traveller to do as he desired. The tourist noticed that the castle was closed, and before he left, asked the gardener, "How long since the owner of the castle was here?"

"About twelve years."

"Does he ever write to you?"

"No."

"Then who gives you your instructions?"

"The master has an agent in Milan."

"Does he ever come here?"

"Never."

The tourist smiled appreciatively and added, "You certainly keep these grounds in excellent condition. They look as if you expected your master to come tomorrow."

The gardener almost interrupted his visitor to say, "Today, sir; today."

MARTHA . . . a woman in a million

(Luke 10:38; John 11:20; 12:2)

Dear Martha,

We have fallen in love with you. No, don't blush. We have no wish to embarrass you, and this is no sudden surge of sentiment. Perhaps you did not realise that you were being watched. Possibly you felt a little overshadowed by your more illustrious sister; but all the time, our eyes have followed you. Dear Martha, do not be upset. We think the world of your lovely sister Mary; but if we had to choose between you, there would hardly be a choice. Martha, you have captured our hearts.

Martha, Who Welcomed the Lord—Luke 10:38

There, dear girl, we feel better now. It took courage to reveal all that was in our hearts; but your smile reassures us. We have not offended; our affection is not unwelcome. Splendid! Martha, we may never have heard of either Mary or Lazarus if you had not first opened your heart and home to Jesus. The Bible declares, " Now it came to pass . . that Jesus entered into a certain village: *and a certain woman named Martha received him into her house.*" Why, had the Master not been permitted to proceed along your street, not a member of your family might have been mentioned in God's great Book. What made you do it, Martha? That invitation brought thirteen extra people to lunch, and if certain dignitaries and neighbours crowded in, you had quite a party! You complained that Mary shirked her duty—Sh, don't tell anyone, we would have complained earlier and longer. Dear Martha, we take our hats off to you, for the Master's gentle rebuke corrected you *for ever.* You never made the same mistake again. Oh Martha, you put us to shame. On an average we would have complained two or three times per day.

Martha, Who Went to the Lord—John 11:20

Yes, you were always the genius in the background. Others at mealtimes said grace, and thanked God for good food. Did they forget that you had cooked it? Dear Martha, so much of God's good food is ruined by bad cooks! First Mary crowded you out, and then Lazarus did likewise. Oh no, we are not complaining. We are glad and thankful that people enthuse over the resurrection of Lazarus; but why are they so blind? You were the only one in the family to retain a balance of faith in those dread days. When your brother was already dead, you said to Jesus, " . . . Lord, if thou hadst been here, my brother had not died. But I know, that even now—*even now*—whatsoever thou wilt ask of God, God will give it thee" (John vv. 21, 22). Martha, you are a gem. "Even now, even now," you said; your faith was smiling through the tears. The deepening corruption of a lifeless body was nothing *if only Jesus would pray*. And yet, Martha, *you did not ask Him to do this*. Of course you wanted Him to pray, but you never asked; for it might not have been God's will to answer according to your desire. You probably thought the loss of your brother was preferable to anything contrary to the will of God. Your eyes said, "If it be Thy will, Lord, please do it for us; but if not, everything will be all right: we will understand." Oh Martha, you wonderful woman.

Martha, Who Worked for the Lord—John 12:2

"Where is Martha?" they often asked; but ultimately they all knew where to find you—in the kitchen. You were not known for your wonderful sermons; you were famous for scones. You were not a specialist in new dresses in which to attend meetings; you were more concerned with a new cloth to spread over the table, and dinners which included the Master's favourite dishes. And when the news came that Simon the Leper intended to entertain the Saviour, you volunteered to help. *"And Martha served."* Yes, yes, we know that Mary sat and heard thrilling sermons—God bless her! Lazarus, graceful, grateful, good, sat near the Master and quietly worshipped. Yes, God bless him too! They were both enjoying a rare spiritual experience at an ancient Keswick convention—while you worked. You would have loved to hear the stories of grace; it would have been refreshingly wonderful if you could have taken off the apron to share the delights of His ministry. Your smiles revealed the content of your heart. You were working for the Lord. That cup you washed would soon touch His lovely lips; the piece of bread you cut would soon rest in the hand that made the world. Yes, and you went into the kitchen, which that night seemed a bit of heaven. Oh, Martha, we must stop now or you will be laughing at us. When love fills the heart it runs away with the tongue; so dear sister, we are leaving before we appear to be foolish. But listen, we give you fair warning. When we come home to heaven, we shall look for you, and, well—be prepared.

Noah's Ark—in the Bathroom

The Sunday-school lesson had been graphically given; the children were spell-bound as the gifted teacher told once again the immortal story of Noah and the flood. It had been easy to visualise the rising waters; the strange vessel with its load of animals; the landing on Mount Ararat; and the final sacrifice when Noah expressed his gratitude to God. Yes, the lesson had been well told, and even the children appeared to be sorry when the time arrived to go home. It was a dismal day, for the rain lashed the streets, making walks or outdoor play impossible. Wrapping their coats around them, a brother and sister hurried home to re-enact what they had just heard. They agreed to play in the bathroom, for the bath was the logical place for a flood, and the shower could supply the rain. An old box was set afloat on the rising waters, and into it were placed many toy animals. Backwards and forwards the old box was pushed, and the youngsters had a rare time. When the bath was nearly full, the children reluctantly decided it was time for the waters to subside, and the girl gently pulled the plug. Slowly the waters descended, until the Ark came to rest on " Mount Ararat." The game was over! Then the boy remembered that after the flood Noah offered a sacrifice; so he seized one of his sister's toys and suggested it should be burnt as a sacrifice. " Oh, no! " said the girl. " You cannot burn that; it is too good. I want it for myself." Lifting one of her brother's toys, she examined it, and said it would make a wonderful sacrifice because it would burn so well. Resolutely Jimmy refused, and soon both children were arguing fiercely. It was only after a heated discussion that they decided neither had much use for an old toy lamb that had lost two legs, both ears, and had no tail. Mutually satisfied, they said, " We will give this to God, for it's no good anyway, and we shall not want it again."

Possibly some will smile at this story, but is there not a danger that even adults can make the same mistake? Centuries ago David said, " . . . neither will I offer burnt-offerings unto the Lord my God of that which doth cost me nothing . . . " (2 Samuel 24:24). So much of our service, offerings, devotion is second-rate: we give to God that which we do not desire. The divine law states, " Give, and it shall be given unto you; good measure, pressed down, and running over " (Luke 6:38). Martha, the woman in a million, always gave her best to Christ: and we should emulate her example.

During my Australian itinerary I visited Parkes, in western New South Wales. My host was a genial Baptist elder who had an intriguing grandson. It was no cause for amazement when the child began to show signs of spiritual interest, for his parents and grandparents were fine Christians. The lad loved attending my services, and made no secret of the fact that my stories to children were far better than my sermons! After a Sunday morning service, the old grandfather came home with a beaming face. Obviously something had pleased him, and I was not surprised when he took me aside to say, " Mr. Powell, that kid is some lad. When you announced that the offering would be received, he put his hand into his pocket and brought out the only two coins he had—a penny and a two-shilling piece (one cent and a quarter). First he gripped one coin, and then the other, and it was obvious he was debating which coin should go into the collection. When the deacon passed the plate, the boy was about to give a penny, but suddenly changing his mind and saying, ' Oh well, I suppose He had better have that one,' he put his two shillings on the plate." I liked the way he said, " *He* had better have that one." Obviously the boy knew his money was being given to Christ, and to offer a mere penny would have seemed unpardonable when a greater gift was possible.

I also knew a boy in New Zealand. When his father gave him a pet sheep, Winstone, with rare business instinct, said, " Dad, is she all mine? And can I have the wool and sell it?" " Yes, my son." When shearing time arrived and the wool was later sold, the boy had difficulty with his arithmetic. He needed help in dividing a difficult sum of money. When his father enquired what it was all about, he was surprised but delighted to know that Winstone wished to give a tenth of his income to God. He knew his father did this, and was determined to follow in Daddy's footsteps.

> What shall I give Thee, Master?
>   Thou Who didst die for me;
> Shall I give less of what I possess,
>   Or shall I give all to Thee?
> Jesus, my Lord and Saviour,
>   Thou hast given all for me;
> Thou didst leave Thy home above
>   To die on Calvary:
> Not just a part or half of my heart:
>   I will give all to Thee.

CHRIST . . . and His chapter of opportunities

(LUKE 13)

There is a strange sequence of thought in the thirteenth chapter of Luke's Gospel, for here three pictures are brought together to form what might be called a composite picture of the evangelical message. That each one of the three is complete in itself, none would deny; but investigation reveals that each one of the trio belongs to its companions. They are meant to contribute to each other, for united they present to mankind the most important message ever told.

Opportunities will not Last for Ever—vv. 6-9

The fig tree seemed a little out of place; many people surely wondered why it was ever allowed to stay. A fig tree in the middle of a vineyard seemed as incongruous as an elephant in a greenhouse! Yet for some inscrutable reason, the owner of the vineyard permitted it to stay. Surely he loved figs! Yet his liking for this fruit gave place to disappointment, and ultimately he said, " Behold, these three years I come seeking fruit on this fig tree, and find none: cut it down; why cumbereth it the ground?" Then the dresser of the vineyard replied, " Lord, let it alone this year also, till I shall dig about it, and dung it: and if it bear fruit, well: and if not, then after that thou shalt cut it down." The vineyard represented the world; the fig tree, the Jewish nation. That God loved the whole world was perfectly understandable, but why He should select the Jewish people to be His chosen race presented problems. A fig tree in the midst of a vineyard! During three years, the Lord sought fruit from the people He loved most; but alas, His expectations were not realised. When Christ said, " Let it alone *this year*," He obviously referred to the fourth year of His own ministry—the year in which He was to die. He was determined to make a final endeavour to influence Jewry, and their destiny would be settled by their reactions to His ministry.

Opportunities can Quickly Pass By—vv. 24-30

The golden sun was setting. Soon the gold would change to pink, and then to scarlet, and finally the ball of glory would sink beyond western horizons. The guardian of the gate stood ready to close the doors; people were hurrying; no camel driver wished to stay outside until sunrise. Beasts were urged to greater speed and the sun sank lower still. A short distance down the road two cameliers animatedly greeted each other. They were old friends; many months had passed since their last meeting. They talked of many things, and time slipped by. Soon a bugle sounded from the gate, and the great doors slowly swung into the closed position. Then the incoming traveller urged his camels to a trot, and approaching the gates cried for admittance. The imperturbable gateman calmly listened to the requests of the visitor and said, " I never knew you. Were you not standing along the road talking? You are well acquainted with our laws; you had an excellent opportunity to enter while the gates were open. Instead you wasted your time talking about things of little consequence. I never knew you." The city could be the Kingdom of God, for as the Lord Jesus described the scene, He said, " Strive to enter in at the strait gate: for many, I say unto you, will seek to enter in, and shall not be able."

Opportunities Lost Seldom Return—vv. 34, 35

The city seemed to be spread out as a cloth at His feet. O place of memories; the city of God, so honoured, so guilty, so loved! And the Lord sighed and said, " O Jerusalem, Jerusalem, which killest the prophets, and stonest them that are sent unto thee; how often would I have gathered thy children together, as a hen doth gather her brood under her wings, and ye would not! Behold, your house is left unto you desolate . . . " We are told that as He saw the city, He wept over it, and described the horrors soon to turn it into a place of unprecedented misery. He spoke of the destruction of the temple, and of the inhuman savagery which would destroy mothers and annihilate a generation even before its birth. And when He saw these things looming in Israel's immediate future, the vision broke His heart. His people had been so near to salvation, but now they had missed it for ever. Never again would that generation be visited by the Son of God; never again would these people hear, " Come unto me, all ye that labour and are heavy laden, and I will give you rest." Israel's opportunity had gone, and even the Lord Himself could not bring it back to them. " And Jesus wept!"

Herein is wisdom. Here is a warning. Our proverb says, " A stitch in time saves nine." A decision in time saves eternity!

Grace Abounding

" Mr. Powell, I'm in trouble." The speaker was a plump little man, obviously agitated. I was surprised, for knowing the man as I did, I had come to believe he was not lacking in self-confidence. Though small of stature, he was capable of ruling the world! " Yes, sir, I'm in great trouble. Will you please try to help me?"

" What is wrong, Mr. ——? "

" My wife has deceived me, sir. I have given her all my wages for months and months, and instead of paying the rent, she has squandered the money. Now the agent for the landlords is turning us out. We have no other place, and you are our only hope. Would you intercede for us and get that man to change his mind? "

" Well, I'll see what I can do. "

The office was small; the agent sat behind his desk. He listened attentively as I stated the purpose of my visit. Mr. and Mrs. —— were very worried. They knew they had been foolish, and wished the agent to give them another chance. I told my tale to the best of my ability, and the agent patiently listened. When I had finished, he quietly said, " Let me show you something, Mr. Powell," and going to a shelf, he reached for a large ledger. " I appreciate what you are trying to do, sir; but now see how utterly unreliable and worthless these people are." He found a certain page, and placing his finger on a long row of figures, outlined what had been happening for three years. He told of promises repeatedly broken, and revealed how the husband was as guilty as the woman he now blamed. " Mr. Powell," he added, " I have been patient; I have gone out of my way to try to help them; I have done all within my power, and now my superiors are putting the squeeze on me. My job is in jeopardy because I have been lenient with scoundrels." I was speechless. This was the other side of the picture. " Mr. Powell, can you give me any good reason why I should not replace these people; why I should not turn them out? " " No, I cannot. I did not know these facts. I am sorry I bothered you." " Good, so you do see my point. All right; there is no earthly reason why I should trust them once more, but I'll do it for your sake. We'll see what happens this time."

Years have passed since that morning, but the people still occupy the same house. The final act of grace was not in vain. I recall the words of Luke 13:7-9, " Behold, these three years I come seeking fruit on this fig tree, and find none: cut it down; why cumbereth it the ground? And he answering said unto him, Lord, let it alone this year also, till I shall dig about it, and dung it: and if it bear fruit, well: and if not, then after that thou shalt cut it down."

The Miracle at Springhill

During October, 1958, the small coal-mining town of Springhill, Nova Scotia, Canada, became a place of tragedy. A " bump " wrecked the number two colliery and entombed about one hundred men. The survivors declared they had often experienced " bumps " when pressure built up in the strata of the earth and "cracked." Yet this upheaval was more like an earthquake. Within seconds the tunnels were wrecked, and even the tram rails were hurled into the roof. Feverishly the rescuers tunnelled through debris in the hope of finding survivors, but as day succeeded day hope was more or less abandoned, and the gloom over the homesteads deepened. The management regretfully announced there could be no chance of men being found alive. Yet the miners refused to give up hope; they said the opportunity of rescuing their comrades would soon be gone; they would continue working until the last possible moment. After a week of unceasing toil the news thrilled the world that ten men had been found alive. Television and radio programmes were changed to permit the entire country to watch and listen as these men were brought to the surface. They had been entombed without food, water and light for a week. The management expressed gratitude to the brave rescuers, but regretfully announced there could be no other survivors. The miners toiled through the night. The following day they found seven other men, and once again the nation rejoiced. Alas, there were no other survivors. The tunnelling men reached the other miners—too late. The old hymn says, " Be in time," and in the rescue of immortal souls, this is the most important truth ever uttered.

LUKE ... who became a connoisseur of pictures

Most men have hobbies, and it would be easy to believe that Dr. Luke was no exception to the rule. Undoubtedly he was a very busy man, yet in his spare time he developed a love for writing; and the quality of his work suggests he would have been an excellent art critic. If his Gospel may be likened to an academy, one may safely say that as an untiring collector he secured many art treasures to hang upon its walls. Some pictures hang alone in splendid isolation; they need neither supporting pictures nor commendation of man. Yet others are strangly related. They hang together, for none are complete without the others. Their production, and even their place in the collection, exhibit genius.

Earth and Its Madness—Luke 14:16-24

The great hall was lavishly decorated; the tables were prepared for a feast that would make history! The host was satisfied. He had planned to honour his guests, and no expense had been spared in supplying the best his wealth could offer. Yet his eyes were becoming shadowy. They were questioning the servants who awaited his instructions. "My lord, I carried your invitation to your friend. He wishes to be excused. He has bought land, and must needs see it." "My lord, I regret to announce that your friend is unable to attend tonight. He has purchased five yoke of oxen, and he declares it is imperative that they be tried out." "My lord, you will be interested to know that your honourable friend has decided to take unto himself a wife. He is very excited, and cannot attend your function." "Then the master of the house being angry said to his servant, Go out quickly into the streets and lanes of the city, and bring hither the poor, and the maimed, and the halt, and the blind ... " The master frowned! An inspection of land; a testing of common beasts; the company of a woman! What trivialities! In considering that picture, Luke was intrigued. That God in Christ should provide a repast of eternal magnificence was beyond his comprehension, but the fact that sinners should invent excuses to refuse God's invitation, suggested madness!

Heaven and Its Gladness—Luke 15:11-24

The night was still; the stars were serene and beautiful. Across the fields, the windows of a farmhouse shone as jewels in a fairy palace. The laughter of the guests announced this to be a night of rejoicing. A long lost son had been found; the wanderer in a far country was home again. Oh, joy! Within the homestead the father's face beamed; he constantly lingered alongside the boy for whom he had waited so long. The guests still remembered the glad cry which echoed from his lips, " Bring forth the best robe, and put it on him; and put a ring on his hand, and shoes on his feet. And bring hither the fatted calf, and kill it; and let us eat and be merry. For this my son was dead, and is alive again; he was lost, and is found." And as Luke carefully placed this picture on the walls of his academy, he remembered the words of the Lord Jesus: " Likewise, I say unto you, there is joy in the presence of the angels of God over one sinner that repenteth " (v. 10). " Whosoever shall confess me before men, him shall the Son of Man also confess before the angels of God " (Luke 12:8). Does this verse explain how the angels are made aware of conversions? The scene beggars description.

Hell and Its Sadness—Luke 16:19-31

Luke's final picture once again brings into bold relief the disgusting people who refused the great invitation. " There was a certain rich man, who was clothed in purple and fine linen, and fared sumptuously every day . . . and he died, and in hell he lifted up his eyes. . . ." The picture is solemn. If this utterance is to be our guide in eternal matters, then certain facts demand consideration. (i) Death is *not* the termination of existence. (ii) Eternity does not destroy one's memory of time. This man remembered his brothers. (iii) Eternity does not provide an opportunity for those who died unrepentant to make a further decision relating to salvation. The man's request for help brought forth the startling response, " . . . between us and you there is a great gulf fixed: so that they who would pass from hence to you *cannot*; neither can they pass to us, that would come from thence." (iv) In all matters relating to this world and the next, the Scriptures stand supreme. If God would not permit the return of a departed soul to warn and evangelise the lost, then the claims of spiritist mediums are false. *If* messages are received from some spirit-world, their origin must be sought in realms not controlled by God. (v) If men desire to prepare for eternity, they should begin immediately. There can be no guarantee that their opportunities will extend until tomorrow.

" I've been an awful fool "

I knew her well, for she was a wealthy business woman in a small town where I often preached. She never attended any church, and excused her action on the grounds that many of her customers came shopping during service hours. Her excuses were many and varied, but occasionally when confronted by the challenge of the Gospel she became angry and said regrettable things. Vehemently she stated that church people should pay their debts, instead of giving money to support lazy clergymen! She was a strange character, completely devoted to the task of increasing her savings. Alas, as the time of her death drew near, her children were amazed when her entire outlook seemed to change. Just before the end, she looked at the family and said, " I hope you will be wiser than your mother. My god has been my money, and what use is it to me now? I never went to church; I ignored the Gospel, and forgot God. I'm dying, and I'm not ready to die. I've been an awful fool. I've made money, but I've lost my soul."

Just in Time

He was a very fine minister, who at one time during his ministry had served as a Police Court Missionary. Some notorious characters had criticised his unflinching loyalty to righteousness, but most of the underworld admitted gratefully that he was a true friend in time of need. One night, the " padre " was accosted by a teenager—one he had never seen previously. She appeared to be ill-at-ease, but there could be no mistaking the evil purpose which had brought her into the night. She was a stranger in the neighbourhood, and had no idea that her first contact was a clergyman. She was most surprised when the man gently but firmly gripped her arm and pushed her into a nearby home. " Who are you? How long have you been here? Who is your boss?" At first she was too frightened to answer, but ultimately his kindly persuasiveness triumphed, and she told all he desired to know. She had quarrelled with her parents, and had run away from her home in the north of England. Penniless, but determined never to return, she had come to the big city, to be introduced to people who promised to help her find employment. Their apparent friendliness only disguised their evil trade, and soon the poor girl was coerced into obeying their commands. Threatened by betrayal to the police on some false charge, she consented to become a prostitute; but the first man she accosted was " the padre." A telegram was sent to the anxious parents, and soon a very grateful father arrived to take his repentent daughter home. The girl's mother had been praying earnestly that God would somehow protect the child, and her prayer had been wonderfully answered.

" Yes, Mr. Powell, she was rescued just in time. I think I can say now that this was the most amazing miracle I ever witnessed." "There is joy in the presence of the angels of God over one sinner that repenteth."

The Ruined Meeting

My old friend the late P.C. Dawes was a fine Christian gentleman, and some of his stories were very effective illustrations. On one occasion he was commissioned to guard the doors of a hall where an atheist was expected to address a large audience. The authorities feared that certain militant Christians might cause trouble, and my friend was instructed to prevent any disturbance. Long afterward he confessed he would have welcomed anything to upset the cold, calculated blasphemy to be uttered on the infidel's platform. Yet he could only stand on guard and pray. Suddenly the door opened, and the policeman was urgently asked to enter. The doorkeeper agitatedly explained that a sudden seizure had prevented the speaker from delivering his address. Would the police come immediately? P.C. Dawes hurried to the platform. He was shocked when he discovered that the lecturer was already dead.

I shall always remember the moments when this fine Christian policeman told me of that strange event. "Yes," he said, "I was standing on those steps wondering what could be done. I would have welcomed any interference, but as an officer of the law I had to preserve the peace. Obviously God would have to fight His own battles! I must confess I did not expect what happened. Surely, God can manage His own affairs—very effectively."

JOHN . . . and his introduction to greatness

The prologue to John's Gospel has always claimed the profoundest attention of Christian students. John was a seer, a mystic. He recognised what others failed to see (cf. 31:7); and his statement, "And there are also many other things which Jesus did, and which, if they should be written every one, I suppose that even the world itself could not contain the books that should be written" (21:25), suggests that he still remembered and treasured details of the Lord's ministry which seemed less important to the other disciples. John's conception of the greatness of Christ surpassed that of all others, and his first chapter supplied a depth of thought unequalled in any other Gospel.

The Word . . . reproducing—vv. 1 and 14

"In the beginning was the Word, and the Word was with God, and the Word was God. . . And the Word was made flesh, and dwelt among us. . . ." No other writer gave this name to Jesus. John recognised that the function of a word is to express the mind of a speaker. Without words, the mind of man would remain inscrutable. Similarly it would have been impossible for man to know God, if God had not expressed Himself. "God . . . hath spoken unto us through his Son" (Heb. 1:1, 2).

The Light . . . revealing—v. 9

It was said of John Baptist, "He was not that Light, but was sent to bear witness of that Light." And the apostle proceeds, "That was the true Light, which lighteth every man that cometh into the world." The suggestion is, that man had lost his way in the dark. The coming of Christ meant that a Light was now shining; it was possible for wanderers to find the way back to God. This was *the true light:* without its guiding beams man would remain lost.

The Christ . . . registering—v. 20

"And John confessed, and denied not; but confessed, I am not the Christ." The coming One would register the fulfilment of all the Messianic predictions. To Him the prophets had pointed, and around Him would revolve all the matters pertaining to the kingdom of God. The Christ would be God's man; the chosen one; the Messiah. John bowed and declared, "I must decrease, he must increase." "I am not the Christ."

The Lamb—redeeming—v. 29

" The next day John seeth Jesus coming unto him, and saith, Behold the Lamb of God, which taketh away the sin of the world." This was another favourite among the names given to Jesus by John. Here we see the magnificent scope of the apostle's vision. Unlike the lambs of the Hebrew penitents—lambs which could only take away the sins of the individual sinners—God's Lamb would make reconciliation for all people. In Him God would redeem the world.

The Son of God . . . representing—v. 34

" And I saw, and bear record that this is the Son of God." Let us never forget that the name " Son " was never given to indicate inferiority to the Father. A son is often greater than his father. This title merely indicates that between son and parent exists an affinity of nature. They belong to the same essence; they are *one* (1:1; 17:5).

The Master . . . receiving—v. 38

" And the two disciples said unto him . . . Master, where dwellest thou? He said unto them, Come and see. They came and saw where he dwelt, and abode with him. . . ." It was destined that the Lamb of God should captivate the affections of human beings; sinners would respond to His charm and follow Him. The key-note of the Lord's ministry was, " Come unto me . . . and him that cometh, I will in no wise cast out."

The King . . . reigning—v. 49

" Nathaniel answered and saith unto him, " Rabbi, thou art the Son of God; thou art the King of Israel." Here is progression of thought. The name *Messiah* suggested that Jesus was the Sent One, sent to establish a kingdom. This new title, *King,* suggests that for Nathaniel at least, the coronation had already taken place. The disciple had crowned his Lord.

The Son of Man . . .remaining—v. 51

This is the fitting climax to John's masterly introduction. Having made the momentous decision to become bone of our bone, and flesh of our flesh, the Lord Jesus is to remain linked with His people for ever. Linked with God and joined to man, He will remain the bridge between human need and divine sufficiency. As the Son of God, He shares in the counsels of the Highest; as the Son of Man, He is acquainted with all our grief and problems. He is the Mediator; the Daysman. He is indispensable both to heaven and earth. Well did Isaiah declare, ". . . and his name shall be called Wonderful " (Isa. 9:6).

The Incomparable Christ

There must be more unofficial christening services in the valleys of Wales than anywhere else on earth. I have no idea how this all began; I only know that now it is the most natural thing for any person suddenly to be given a nickname which will stick closer than glue! More often than not this will refer to an occupation, an infirmity, or to some event with which the person has been connected. Names such as Evans the Milk, Ianto Smallcoal, Billy Baldhead are commonplace. Probably they provide a line of demarcation between that particular person and others whose Christian names are identical. I knew a fine Christian who worked as a pumpsman in the local colliery; he was known as Tommy the Pump. I knew another fine Christian whose finger would not bend; he was known throughout the district as Jimmy Straightfinger. Alas, the name Jenkins is more often than not twisted to Shinkins, and a shoemaker with that name would be Shinkins the Shoe. I knew a man who once wore a top hat to a funeral, until the day of his death he was called Billy Boxhat. Wales is a great country, and for those who know how to appreciate humour, it can be a paradise.

The giving of such expressive names has been known in higher and perhaps more official circles. There have been times in history when some outstanding person revealed characteristics which demanded recognition. King Richard of England was known throughout the realm as Richard the Lion-Heart. A typical Englishman has often been called John Bull, and many other examples might be cited. One of the finest characters in modern times has been the grand old man of the House of Commons, Sir Winston Churchill. He has been given six or seven such names, for this great statesman succeeded in spreading his personality over an Empire. There are millions of people who believe that Great Britain, and indeed the world, will always be indebted to the indomitable war-time Prime Minister.

Yet supreme in the world stands Jesus. His influence was so vast, His gifts so varied, that prophets and writers of all ages borrowed many titles to express what they wished to say about Him. A little while ago, I collected my reference books and deliberately set out to discover how many Biblical titles had been given to the Saviour. I was astounded to discover that within the pages of Holy Scripture between eighty and ninety names had been given to the Son of God.

The door; the vine; the good shepherd; the bread of life; the Messiah; the King of Israel; the carpenter; the author of faith; these are only some of the dozens to be found; and when to the Bible names are added the innumerable titles given by the world's best writers and thinkers, the total

123

becomes great indeed. Yet each name reveals that particular aspect of the life of Jesus which appealed especially to the individual. At the most, twelve titles would be sufficient to express everything about the greatest statesman, poet, scientist, or benefactor the human race has ever produced. The one exception is Jesus of Nazareth, for as long as time shall last, He will remain the Altogether Lovely One. The first chapter of John's Gospel reveals John's conception of his Lord. Within the compass of fifty-one verses, the apostle mentions eight names in addition to the one by which He was known in Nazareth. John was a seer, but it is doubtful whether he ever saw more than a very small part of the exceeding greatness of his Master.

The *Watchman-Examiner,* one of the most influential religious papers in American Church life, has expressed this point perfectly. " His birth was contrary to the laws of life. His death was contrary to the laws of death. He had no cornfields nor fisheries, but He could spread a table for five thousand and have bread and fish to spare. He walked on no beautiful carpets of velvet rugs, but He walked on the waters of the sea of Galilee, and they supported Him. Three years He preached His Gospel. He wrote no book; built no church house; had no monetary backing. But after nineteen hundred years, He is the one central character of human history, the Pivot around which the events of the ages revolve, and the one and only Regenerator of the human race.

" Was it merely the son of Joseph and Mary who crossed the world's horizon nineteen hundred years ago? Was it merely human blood that was spilled at Calvary's hill for the redemption of sinners? What thinking man can keep from exclaiming, ' My Lord and my God? ' ".

THE WORD . . . Who came, and will come again from Outer Space

(JOHN 1:1-14; 1 JOHN 5:7; REVELATION 19:11-16)

The previous chapter suggested that John loved to call Christ "The Word." The apostle believed that Jesus fully expressed the mind of God, and preferred this title above all others. Altogether he wrote five New Testament books, but this theme links them together. On three occasions the apostle wrote of The Word, and the purpose of this study is to bring these Scriptures into bold relief.

In the Gospel . . . The Word Who took man's place—
John 1:1, 18

"No man hath seen God at any time; the only begotten Son, which is in the bosom of the Father, *he hath declared him.*" God is no longer the inscrutable One; no longer is He to be distant and remote, for He has expressed Himself in the Person of the Son. Christ declared that: (i) *God loves.* Against the awe-inspiring background of Sinai, where divine law thundered against sin; after the numerous occasions when righteousness destroyed the guilty, the fact that God loved was a thrilling revelation. (ii) *God gave.* "For God so loved the world, that he gave his only begotten Son. . . ." The Word was made flesh, and dwelt among us. It was almost incomprehensible that the King of angels should become man and be identified with sinners; it was almost unbelievable that He Who was so rich should become so poor; but He did. "He humbled himself, and became obedient unto death, even the death of the cross." (iii) *God offers.* ". . . that whosoever believeth in him should not perish, but have everlasting life." This message superseded anything ever taught by the rabbis. It was in the mind of God that man should share His life and be made partakers of the divine nature, but this would have remained an eternal secret had not God expressed Himself through the Word.

*In the Epistles . . . The Word of heavenly grace—*1 John 5:7

As the Church developed and spread through the world, error began to destroy its unity; and before John went to join his Lord, he felt constrained to issue stern warnings against those who menaced the Christian faith. Aware of the presence of men who denied that the Word had come in the flesh, he denounced their teaching and reaffirmed what he knew to be true. "For there are three that bear record in heaven, the Father, the Word, and the Holy Ghost: and these three are one." The entire passage speaks of the *truth;* the *witness;* the *record.* " And this is the record, that God hath given to us eternal life, and this life is in his Son. He that hath the Son hath life; and he that hath not the Son of God hath not life " (vv. 11, 12). The Gospel was the truth of God expressed through the Son, and rejection of its message was blasphemy, for it made God to be a liar. Although men denied its teaching, a Triune Witness in heaven eternally vindicated the message. As the Word, in heaven Jesus expressed a three-fold fact. (i) He had indeed been offered, for His hands were scarred. (ii) His sacrifice had been accepted, for God had exalted Him to power. (iii) His ministry at God's right hand was effective, for sinners were being accepted. His being where He was, proclaimed that He had not died in vain. God acknowledged this; Christ expressed it; and the Holy Spirit came down to earth to proclaim it.

In the Revelation . . . the Word from outer space—
Revelation 19:11-16

" And I saw heaven opened, and behold a white horse; and he that sat upon him was called Faithful and True, and in righteousness he doth judge and make war. His eyes were as a flame of fire, and on his head were many crowns. . . . And he was clothed in a vesture dipped in blood: and his name is called The Word of God. And the armies which were in heaven followed him upon white horses . . . and out of his mouth goeth a sharp sword, that with it he should smite the nations. . . ." We live in an age when the exploration of outer space seems to be the chief concern of many scientists. Mighty rockets propel sputniks of ever-increasing size into the sky, and plans are being made for space stations from which it is hoped man will be able to explore distant planets. There is reason to believe that before this happens, Christ will return to earth. It is noteworthy that in expounding this truth, John retained the same title. (i) This endorsed the message of the Gospel, for " he was clothed with a vesture *dipped in blood*." (ii) It endorsed His greatness in heaven, for " . . . the armies which were in heaven followed him upon white horses. . . ." (iii) It endorsed the righteousness of God, for " . . . out of his mouth goeth a sharp sword, that with it he should smite the nations. . . ." The Lord Jesus Christ is to return to earth; but for some people this event will be disastrous. Radio and television announcers may work over-time; newspapers may be printed in many editions; statesmen may panic and resign, but *Christ will be here.* This could take place very soon; and if this should be the case, days of opportunity to get right with God may be very few. *Be in time.* While the voice of mercy calls you—*be in time.*

Reflecting Mirrors

During June, 1957, my wife and I took my mother on her first trip overseas. We went to Italy, and for a few delightful weeks travelled through that entrancing country. Milan, Florence, Rome, Naples, Venice: these and many other cities were included in our itinerary, and in every place well-informed guides introduced to us the gems of Italian art. I can never express the superlative magnificence of the churches; Michaelangelo's paintings and carvings beggared description, and the catacombs carried us back to times when persecution drove the Christians underground. We saw so many works of art painted on lofty ceilings that finally we developed a pain in the neck! We shuddered when the guide explained how the famous painter had lain on his back for four years in order to paint one ceiling. Yet in the Rospigliosi palace in Rome, we appreciated the thoughtfulness of the authorities who recognised the strain of looking upward. "The Aurora" is truly a masterpiece, and in order that visitors may view the great painting in comfort, a reflecting mirror has been placed near the door. In this the work of art can be clearly seen, and tired viewers can sit at ease to study every detail of the painter's craft. It is doubtful whether the finer points of the picture would ever be noticed without the help of the mirror.

The Cheddar Caves in England are famous, and to visit them is to enjoy an unforgettable experience. I have seen caves elsewhere in the world, but none excelled those in Britain. A small but beautiful cave is at the lower end of the gorge. This is well worth a visit; but higher up the valley are the larger caves in which is *The Swiss Village.* The guide leads along the darkened passages, and at intervals stops to indicate an ornate piece of Nature's handiwork. Finally he pauses at a small font-like rock, and invites his listeners to look into the pool placidly resting in the shallow depression. There, mirrored perfectly in the water is the reflection of innumerable stalactites. At first it is almost impossible to escape the conclusion that this has been arranged by a clever technician, for in the water is a picturesque village. The church with its steeple is clearly defined; the small winding streets with houses on both sides are seen in bold relief: the sight is truly entrancing. Without the aid of the reflecting waters, that particular piece of roof would be just another piece of rock upon which the sediment of the ages had left a deposit. The placid pool reflects the wonder of the unknown, and is certainly one of Cheddar's greatest treasures.

Both the mirror in Rome and the pool in Cheddar remind us of Christ. It would hardly be possible for sinners to gaze into the face of the Almighty. Eyes would be strained, the vision blurred, the feet unsteady. Travellers in this world would probably proceed on their journey completely ignorant of eternal beauties, had not God decided to reveal Himself. Christ is the mirror; in Him is reflected all the fullness of the Godhead. At His feet we may sit and watch; into the depth of His character we may gaze to see the beauties of the Infinite. And this is precisely the reason why John called Jesus *the Word*. The Saviour was the means—the mirror—the pool—the message by which God chose to reveal Himself.

The Dentist's Wife

She was very small, very efficient, very pretty, but very puzzled. Her husband had been won for Christ three nights earlier, and his overflowing happiness had attracted his intellectual wife. Yes, she would like to be a Christian, but certain things baffled her. Jesus of Nazareth was certainly a very fine man, but how in the wide world could I conscientiously say He was God? Had he not been born of human parents? Had he not lived as a man, worked as a man, and finally died as a man? His example was superb, but to say He was divine—well! I indicated the opening verses of John's Gospel, and when she read, " And the Word was God," I asked if she would tell me of what earthly use was a word. She seemed a little surprised that I should ask such an elementary question, but when I persisted in my enquiry, she explained that without words man would be unable to express himself. Then I asked how God could reveal Himself, or how could any other reveal God? Who, in any case, could reveal God without first having access to the mind of God? It is hardly possible to impart something one does not possess. Suddenly her eyes shone; she was beginning to understand how Jesus came to be a reflecting mirror; that He Who shared the counsels of the Highest was able to express them. Within moments we were kneeling at His feet.

JOHN . . . who remembered how Jesus said, "Come"

(JOHN 1:39; 7:37; 21:12)

I like to think of John as he paused, pen in hand, during the writing of his Gospel. Scenes of bygone days were as clear as if they had happened on the previous day. The Master had been a perfect host, Who loved to share His company. Christ's invitations as recorded in John's Gospel suggest a highway to spiritual blessing.

Come and See . . . a great pleasure—John 1:39

The Jordan valley was a scene of activity, for many people had arrived to hear the wilderness preacher. " And John stood, and two of his disciples; and looking upon Jesus as he walked, he saith, Behold the Lamb of God. And the two disciples heard him speak, and they followed Jesus. Then Jesus turned . . . and saith unto them, What seek ye? They said unto him . . . Master, where dwellest thou? He saith unto them, Come and see. They came and saw where he dwelt, and abode with him. . . ." How we would love to talk to those disciples. What did Jesus say during their stay in His home? Did he make any prediction or expound any Scripture? Did He prepare a meal, and if so, what did they eat? There are so many things we would like to know. " One of the two was Andrew. . . . He findeth his own brother Simon, and saith unto him, We have found the Messiah." Three things are apparent. (i) He heard Christ's invitation, and accepted it. (ii) His coming to Christ brought assurance to his own soul. (iii) His increasing enthusiasm begat an intense desire to bring others to the Lord. This sequence of events is always reproduced with every true conversion.

Come and Drink . . . a great promise—John 7:37

The supply of water in the city of Jerusalem was always a major problem, and at feast-time it became a menace. When thousands of visitors invaded the capital, it was impossible to meet the demands made upon the meagre supplies. The last day of the feast always brought restrictions, and requests for water were made everywhere. Thus, it was truly astounding when Jesus stood and cried, " If any man thirst, let him come unto me, and drink." The Master obviously chose the time for His most challenging utterance; but as the people surged in His direction, they became disappointed to discover that this was not exactly what they desired. Undoubtedly some complained about His remarks, but with calm deliberation he added: " He that believeth on me, as the scripture hath said, out of his inner man shall flow rivers of living water." Long afterward John remembered this speech and explained, " But this spake he of the Spirit, which they that believe on him should receive: for the Holy Ghost was not yet given; because that Jesus was not yet glorified." This second invitation of Christ seems to link with the desire of Andrew to win his brother. When thirsty souls discover the wells of God's salvation, they have an increasing desire to share their satisfaction with others. The soul is more than a receptacle—it becomes a channel! The living water first flows into the human heart, and then through it to a waiting world. John declared the water was a symbol of the Holy Spirit, and the Scriptures suggest three things: (i) *salvation*—He meets my need; (ii) *sanctification*—He fills me; (iii) *service*—He uses me.

Come and Dine . . . a great provision—John 21:12

The beach was still; the silence was unbroken except for the sound of the waves and the sudden squawk of a bird. The Saviour was about to serve breakfast to His tired guests. They looked at His kind and dignified face, and remembered the invitation with which He had welcomed them: "Come and dine." A night's fruitless toil had left them weary and discouraged, but when their task seemed to be completely hopeless, His appearance on the beach had turned defeat into triumph. He had kindled a fire and invited them to breakfast. At that fireside they were to discover new strength which would enable them to meet the demands of the future. Long afterward, Peter remembered that morning; and when John was old, he could still recall all that happened. They sat on the beach while the Master healed the wounds in their spirit. Probably they remembered, too, that other occasion when after a period of itinerant preaching they had returned to hear the Lord say, " Come ye yourselves apart . . . and rest a while . . ." (Mark 6:31). Service is a great privilege, but to commune with Christ is far better. To be alone with the Master means a new appreciation of: (i) *His power*—He, too, can catch fish—many of them. (ii) *His purpose*—it is then that He issues His commands, " Feed my sheep," etc. (iii) *His* person—surpassing the joy of service is the glory of His presence. It is heaven to be at His feet. " Come and see " is enrolment in God's school. " Come and drink " is proficiency in study. " Come and dine " is to graduate; and only then is the Master truly satisfied with His student.

The Indian's Parable

During my itinerary of Western Canada I conducted evangelistic meetings in the Baptist church at Penticton, and it was there that, for the second time, I met the Rev. Gordon Vincent. Exactly twelve months earlier I had missioned in his former church at Woodstock, New Brunswick; and as a result of campaigning twice with the same minister, I came to know him very well. Mr. Vincent had one of the largest libraries I had ever seen, and suspecting that he possessed hidden stores of excellent illustrations, I asked if he could give me a good story. His kindly eyes sparkled as he scanned his many books. Possibly he suspected that I had great interest in native peoples; my travel films of New Guinea, Africa, Australia, and New Zealand had all supplied evidence of that fact. It was not surprising, therefore, when he informed me about the Indian's parable.

During a Gospel meeting, an Indian and a white man had been convicted of sin. The Word of God had disturbed them to such an extent that both were exceedingly miserable. The Indian surrendered himself to Christ, and became supremely happy; his white brother went away distressed. Several weeks passed, and finally the second man became a Christian, and rejoiced in the forgiveness of sin. Then he remembered the weeks of weariness during which he had almost despaired of finding peace. All this puzzled him, and when he met the Indian Christian, he shared his thoughts. " My brother, I wonder why it was that you found happiness in one night, while I had to wait many weeks to get it? " The Indian smiled and replied, " Me tell you. There was a great prince, who was very wealthy. When he met us, he was sorry for us, and offered us his wonderful coat. Now you had a very nice suit, which had cost much money. You looked at your suit and thought, ' I do not need his coat. I am well dressed.' Now me, I no well dressed. I look at my poor blanket, which is no good anyhow, and I say, His coat is good; he give it to me as a present. Me take it. I make up mind soon, for I am poor. You think and think and think, for you believe you not poor. That's why you miserable."

A Penny for Bobbie

Charles Haddon Spurgeon bequeathed to mankind some of the best stories ever told, and among the number was that of an orphan called Bobbie. Mr. Spurgeon describing the incident says, " Sitting down in the orphanage grounds upon one of the seats, I was talking with one of our brother trustees, when a little fellow about eight years of age left the other boys who were playing around us, and came deliberately up to us. He opened fire upon us thus, ' Please, Mr. Spurgeon, I want to come and sit down upon that seat between you two gentlemen.'

' Come along, Bob, and tell us what you want.'

' Please, Mr. Spurgeon, suppose there was a little boy who had no father, who lived in an orphanage with a lot of other little boys who had no fathers, and suppose those little boys had mothers and aunts who comed once a month, and brought them apples and oranges, and gave them pennies, and suppose this little boy had no mother and no aunts, and so nobody never came to give him nice things; don't you think somebody ought to give him a penny? 'Cause, Mr. Spurgeon, that's me! ' "

The Shepherd's Call

The Rev. Griffith Thomas has described a scene well known to people who have travelled in the Middle East. He had been watching a number of shepherds watering their flocks, and marvelling at the way in which thousands of animals from various directions all mingled until a surging mass of sheep jostled and struggled around the watering place. He saw the shepherds unconcernedly talking to each other, and not in the least worried about the task of separating their animals from the struggling throng. Mr. Thomas wondered how the seeming miracle would be performed; but when the time of departure arrived, each shepherd went his way calling to his sheep. Instantly the animals responded to the call, and without any confusion followed their master. Intrigued by the situation, Mr. Thomas overtook one of the shepherds and asked a question. "Do your sheep always follow you like that? " " Yes, sir, they know my voice, and when I call to them, they always follow me." Mr. Thomas thought for a while and then asked, " Have you ever known a time when they did not respond to your voice? " The shepherd answered, " Yes, there is a time when the sheep will not respond. When a sheep is sick, it will follow anybody. But as long as the animal is healthy, it will always respond to the call of its own shepherd." Surely, many people must be sick!

PENTECOST . . . the miracle that staggered a world

(Acts 2)

Pentecost changed the world; without it, the Church would have been another sect destined to disappear within a few months. The Saviour expressed superlative truth when He said, " It is expedient for you that I go away: for if I go not away, the Comforter will not come unto you. . . ." (John 16:7.) Even now as in retrospect we review the whole proceeding, it seems utterly fantastic that unlearned and inexperienced men should attempt to overthrow the teaching of centuries; to challenge heathen strongholds, and then to evangelise a world with the astounding news that a Carpenter nailed to a cross had been the Son of the Living God. Not one member of the original twelve had been trained in theology; not one was a polished speaker. They were rough, blunt men drawn from ordinary walks of life; but Pentecost transformed midgets into giants!

Power to Perceive

Just before the Lord ascended to heaven, He said to the disciples, " Ye shall receive power, after that the Holy Spirit is come upon you: and ye shall be witnesses unto me. . . ." The scope of this promise is far wider than one would at first imagine. During the Lord's ministry, the disciples thought only of an earthly kingdom, and all their preaching expressed self-desire. The writings of the prophets were never fully understood; some of the most outstanding utterances were treated as commonplace. Pentecost changed the entire outlook of these men. Ancient parchments came alive within their minds; the Lamb of God was recognised as the Lamb slain from before the foundation of the world; the Old Testament sacrifices were seen as types and shadows of the Gospel revelation. Their amazement gave place to wonder, and a new perception inspired their oft-repeated utterance, " Thus was it fulfilled which was written by the prophets " (see John 16:13).

Power to Prevail

Actions speak louder than words. It was obvious that if these fishermen were to succeed in their tremendous task, they needed more than intellectual illumination. Simon Peter possessed a volcanic soul! He could be a flaming fury, or a dormant despondent. *Within* these men lived their greatest enemies. It was possible to denounce the evil of passion and at the same time to be a victim of a vile temper. It was possible to pronounce a curse on adultery and yet to harbour secretly lustful thoughts. No man should ever preach beyond his experience. The disciples needed power to trample under foot the very evils by which they themselves had been overcome; and if Simon Peter, so recently scared by a maiden, were to stand unafraid before an immense crowd of potential murderers, then he needed a new dynamic to banish completely his former timidity. Pentecost supplied that essential. The coming of the Holy Spirit made it possible for the power of God to be known in human weakness. God through the Holy Spirit did for man what self-effort could never do.

Power to Preach

". . . and ye shall be witnesses unto me both in Jerusalem, and in all Judaea, and in Samaria, and unto the uttermost part of the earth." Pentecost changed a hesitant, half-hearted company of believers into a machine capable of making hell tremble. Probably Simon Peter preached many hundreds of times during those memorable tours when in company with another disciple he had gone forth to announce the nearness of the kingdom. Yet, in spite of all his sincere efforts, there is no record that he ever won a soul for his Master. Undoubtedly he tried hard; of course he put his best into all his efforts, but success in soul-winning seemed utterly elusive. His hearers seemed to be clothed in impenetrable indifference. Then, without any unique preparation, this same preacher saw three thousand souls yielding to Christ in one service. Even Peter was surely astounded. No one could claim that his effort represented perfection in preaching. There was nothing particularly attractive about his phraseology. The secret lay not in Peter's artistry, but in the unmistakable power which turned every sentence into an arrow reaching human hearts. Without Pentecost the disciples would have been just another band of workers who after a few short years of ministry would have retired to some obscure parish in the country! Instead, they became living flames! Their preaching kindled a bush fire which swept across continents. Pentecost changed the world; and another Pentecost could do it again.

He had New Blood in his Veins!

I shall never forget the first time I saw a game of American football; it seemed the craziest spectacle I had ever witnessed. I was completely bewildered, and so were my friends who failed to appreciate my caustic comments. When the players appeared they looked like the shock troops of a crack regiment; highly trained commandos anxious to annihilate the opposition. Each man had a helmet, and shoulders padded to withstand the fury of charging tanks! When the ball was set in motion, the fellows charged like bulls; and about every fifteen seconds the game was interrupted to permit the forwards to retire to a committee meeting a few yards up the field. It was the queerest sight I had ever seen in any sporting engagement; but when I turned to observe the crowd, they all seemed in perfect agreement with the committee business. When I asked why the players were constantly going into a huddle like a lot of old women, I was informed that this was an essential part of football technique. During the moments of isolated huddle, the captain or chief conspirator confided to his companions in crime what the next move should be. To me it was all so strange, and I confess that even now I have not the least idea what it was all about. Yet I shall always be glad that I saw such games, for with them came the delightful story of a very small football enthusiast.

Each evening, alongside the football field of an American university, a small boy excitedly watched the players practising. Constantly he followed the play up and down the touchline, and his chatter amused the fellows. They all knew him, and appreciated the fact that he idolised the star quarterback. It became a nightly occurrence for the child to describe all he had seen at the playing field, and to add, " Dad, when I get big, I'm going to be a quarter-back just like Bill Jones." Then came the evening when the youthful enthusiast did not appear at the practice game, and the players wondered what had detained him. When they heard that the boy had been rushed to hospital, and that an urgent blood transfusion was necessary to save his life, all volunteered to give blood. Among them was found one man with the correct blood group, and his willingness to help saved the child's life. Some time later, when the lad had recovered sufficiently to be taken home, his father tried to cheer him by saying, " It won't be long now before you can see the fellows practising, and learn how to become the greatest quarter-back in the country." He was astounded when his son replied, " Dad, I can't be a quarter-back. I have the blood of a tackle in me now, and I will have to be the greatest tackle in the country."

This delightful story perfectly illustrates the amazing exploits of the early Church. Probably the disciples had ideas and ambitions of their own, yet after Pentecost all these became subordinate to a tremendous desire. They realised that the life of Another had come into their beings; that the greatest transfusion possible had saved them from the dangers of sin. The Holy Spirit had filled them with the life of Christ, and as a direct result of this miracle, all their personal plans were changed. As they went out to the great playing fields of experience, their one desire was to emulate the example of Him whose life they had received. When they succeeded gloriously the citizens of Antioch recognised the achievement, and from that moment the disciples were called *Christians*.

Free Air

The sign "Free Air" is always a welcome sight to the motorist whose tyres are flat. Only those unfortunate drivers who have had punctures far from a garage know the drudgery of pumping by hand. The continuous up and down movements on the handle of a pump, the increasing ache in that part of the back where it hurts, the lingering feeling that the desired pressure will never be reached—these are among the lesser joys of motoring. Yet the offer of free air brings sparkle to weary eyes, relief to aching backs; and a drudgery becomes delight as limitless supplies pour into a deflated tyre.

Christian service can also become a heartache, a discouraging experience, when the innumerable ups and downs of daily events seem to be getting us nowhere. We are told that God has limitless supplies of mighty power, but the problem remains how we may connect our weakness with His might. It is cheering to know that "God's Service Stations" are everywhere; no traveller need be stranded far from a source of help. A sense of weakness, a bended knee, a sincere petition, an absolute reliance upon the Divine Spirit—these connect us to unfailing resources of power. Yet we must remember that even free air may be hindered by dirty, sticking valves. Let us be sure that our contacts with Him are clean and unresisting, and through the power of a personal Pentecost we shall laugh at impossibilities.

THE CHURCH ... on a rising tide

(ACTS 4:33; 8:8)

Pentecost, coming exactly seven weeks and a day after Passover, perfectly fulfilled the ancient types set in the Jewish feasts. It also fulfilled the mighty promises given by the prophets of successive generations. Pentecost liberated currents of supernatural power, and the early chapters of the Acts reveal a rising tide of spiritual dynamic.

Great Power—Acts 4:33

There is a preaching which bores the listener; which reminds one that the seats are hard, the service too long, and the outside world a most desirable place. There is a preaching which thrills the soul, convicts of sin, and begets increasing determination to go forth to be better men and women. After the coming of God's Spirit, the disciples with great power spoke of the resurrection of their Lord; and immediately a miracle took place within the hearts of those who listened.

Great Grace—Acts 4:33

Preaching which appeals only to the intellect is useless. To be of value, a man's message must reach the hidden depths of human nature. New Testament preaching not only stirred hearts; it tamed passions and loosened purse strings. People who possessed land, sold it in order to place the proceeds in the common treasury. They had obviously become acquainted with John's teaching: " But whoso hath this world's goods, and seeth his brother have need, and shutting up his bowels of compassion from him, how dwelleth the love of God in him? " (1 John 3:17).

Great Fear—Acts 5:11

The hypocrisy of Ananias and Sapphira produced an ominous cloud in an otherwise cloudless sky. Their deliberate decision to lie to the Church leaders constituted a crime; and since holiness never fails to reveal and rebuke hypocrisy, the offenders died. "Who shall ascend into the hill of the Lord? He that hath clean hands. . . ."

A true revival never needs advertising. " And great fear came upon . . . as many as heard these things."

Great Wonders and Miracles—Acts 6:8

The growing Church soon discovered the need for conse-crated leaders. God's business should never be done in a half-hearted, slipshod way. Consecrated men were appointed to control the various organisations and committees, and the first requisite in connection with these leaders was spirituality. "And Stephen, full of faith and power, did great wonders and miracles among the people." Happy is that church whose deacons are able to perform miracles! Could these things happen today? Would it still be possible for the sick to be healed by men filled with the Spirit of God? The answer to that question can only be *yes*. Much of what passes now for divine healing is dissatisfying and fraudulent. The way modern healers man-handle their patients sometimes borders on the disgusting. Nevertheless, if we believe the Scriptures we must agree that anything is possible when the Church moves in the centre of the will of God.

Great Joy—Acts 8:8

Persecution increased the discomfort of the early Christians, but it failed to destroy their happiness. "Therefore they that were scattered abroad went everywhere preaching the word. Then Philip went down to the city of Samaria, and preached Christ unto them . . . and there was great joy in that city." A miserable Christian broadcasts to the world that something has gone wrong with his Christianity. Shadows on the face mean a cloud on the sun. The first indication that a life has been filled with the power of God is seen when that life overflows with radiant happiness. The charm of the Gospel, the power of the preaching, the unity of the believers, the increasing challenge to unbelievers: these characteristics always deepen devotion and increase the joy of the redeemed.

After years of apathetic indifference, when the cause of God had been at a low ebb, Pentecost turned the tide, and soon lives which had been derelict, stranded, and abandoned, were brought within the harbour of God's love. Our greatest need today is another Pentecost.

My Mother's Clocks

During May, 1958, a cablegram from Wales announced that my mother had been called home to heaven, and for two months my Canadian itinerary had to be interrupted. Ultimately it became necessary to sell my home, and in listing the things for sale, I found my mother's clocks. She had a considerable collection, and I had many frustrating moments making them acceptable to customers. I shall never forget the little clock on which the hands were constantly sticking. Apparently the works were in good order; they "ticked" all right: but just when I was satisfied the clock was in perfect condition, the hands took hold of each other and refused to be separated. Then I found another timepiece which my mother had pushed into the back of a drawer. I wondered why she had discarded the thing, for it was rather attractive; but when I wound it, a remarkable thing happened. Buzzing like an infuriated bee, the works announced they were in great haste and the hands went round at breakneck speed. Let me hasten to confess I am not a watchmaker; I know nothing about the mechanism of clocks, and consequently had no idea what was wrong. Round and round flew the hands, in support of the text that a thousand years are as a day. Then quite suddenly the buzzing ceased and the hands stopped. When I wound the clock again, for the second time it went mad! Finally I put it aside, for it was either motionless or running for its life! I could do nothing with it. Then I came to a small mantel-clock which was unquestionably beautiful. Its polished surface suggested a thing of worth, and I realised it would not be difficult to find a buyer. I wound and placed it in a central position above the fireplace; but when I went into the room a little later, the clock had stopped. I shook it, and it started again. Within the next fifteen minutes I returned again, and was thrilled to see it behaving itself! Yes, I had made a good job of it—but a little later it had stopped once more. Annoyed, I bumped it rather roughly, and the clock responded magnificently. This time it went for thirty minutes, but then stopped. When I placed a little wedge beneath one end of the clock, my annoying little friend appreciated my interest and suitably responded. After twenty minutes it stopped once more. When I put the wedge the other side, my efforts were again rewarded —for a time. Finally I reached the place where the clock responded each time I bumped it, but ultimately I gave it "good measure, pressed down and running over" and it stopped for ever!

Yes, my dear mother had many clocks; big ones and small ones, tall ones and short ones, fat clocks, alarm clocks, wall clocks. Yet she never had an electric clock. I had one, and it was superb! It never uttered any roaring summons; it never made any fuss. Its hands never went racing ahead; its works never came to a stop. The clock was connected with power, and kept perfect time. It was worth its weight in gold! When I awakened in the night, I looked at my bedside friend, and there shining in the darkness was its radiant face. The gloom only accentuated its illumined dial; and although the clock never uttered a sound, it told me the time as eloquently as any orator could have done.

Those clocks remind me of the Church. There are many nice people who " tick " all right and are a joy to behold. They never cause trouble unless they are asked to do something; then their hands " stick." There are others who are most annoying. They are either very cold or exceedingly hot. They never attend a meeting in six months, or they live on the pastor's doorstep complaining the church is asleep! Their spiritual life is a series of jerks—revivals; but between each one is a period of indifference when they do little for the kingdom of God. There are others who are excellent workers if someone constantly chases them. Without a bump they seldom respond, and of course, the danger is ever present that if they get bumped too hard, they might stop for ever! I shall always thank God that within the one and only church I ever had, were very wonderful people. They did not send out alarms announcing their presence and demanding attention; they never caused trouble. Constantly they were plugged into the power lines of heaven, and living energy flowed into their beings. They were utterly dependable, and quite valuable to their young minister. Their lights shone forth into the darkness, and men saw their good works and gave praise to God. Nearly all the early churchmen were of this type, and that was the reason why they turned the world upside down.

THE ETHIOPIAN EUNUCH . . . to whom we would send a letter

(ACTS 8:26-40)

Dear Sir,

You may not be aware of the fact, but your story has fascinated millions of readers. It suggests romance and mystery of the highest order; it brings to the mind the dark forests of Ethiopia, the glittering splendour of an ancient court where you served, and hints at all kinds of vague possibilities as to why you went on a long journey to worship the God of another race. It is more than likely that you were an Ethiopian, a dark-skinned man of Africa. How, then, did you become acquainted with Israel's God? Had some travelling trader told you of the new, or should I say the old, faith? Had you travelled and studied in other lands? It has been suggested that you were a Hebrew and, as many of your countrymen, had found favour in a royal house of another nation. There are so many things we would like to mention; but since these ordinary questions have so often been asked, forgive us if we confine our interests to the more unusual type of enquiry. Your journey to Jerusalem, your subsequent meeting with Philip the evangelist, and your surrender to Jesus Christ, are very well known. Probably you often delighted your friends with your testimony. We are wondering if the broader implications of this miracle have passed unnoticed.

God's Faithfulness

Perhaps in your moments of reminiscence, you marvelled that a stranger should have met you on a desert highway. Really, sir, the event was a direct answer to prayer. Did you know that long before you were born, King Solomon prayed for you? Let us quote from the ancient record, ". . . Moreover concerning a stranger, that is not of thy people Israel, but *cometh out of a far country for thy name's sake* (For they shall hear of thy great name, and of thy strong hand, and of thy stretched-out arm); *when he shall come and pray toward this house; Hear thou in heaven* thy dwelling place, and do according to all that the stranger calleth to thee for . . . " (1 Kings 8:41-43). God is faithful; His covenant promises assure His people that He will answer prayer. No one agency alone is responsible for conversion. Believing prayer is a bridge thrown across the centuries.

God's Righteousness

Dear friend from Africa, you must be proud of the fact that long before your day, another Ethiopian rendered salutary service to a prophet of the true God. Once again let us quote from the ancient writings. "Now when Ebed-melech the Ethiopian, one of the eunuchs which was in the king's house, heard that they had put Jeremiah in the dungeon . . . he went forth out of the king's house, and spake to the king. . . . So Ebed-melech . . . took thence old cast clouts and old rotten rags, and let them down by the cords into the dungeon to Jeremiah. . . . So they drew up Jeremiah, and took him out of the dungeon" (Jer. 38:7-13). God has a wonderful way of paying debts. There had been an occasion when an Ethiopian rendered service to a prophet, and probably saved his life; now a prophet was to render service to an Ethiopian, and save his soul.

God's Watchfulness

Have you ever watched an ant moving amongst thousands of others on an anthill? Close your eyes for a second, and it is quite impossible to find the tiny creature. Sir, we have always marvelled that in spite of the fact that millions and millions of people move upon the face of the earth, *God saw you*. God's watchfulness is so wonderful that an individual is never lost in a crowd. Perhaps it was the consciousness of this fact which enabled Job to exclaim, "He knoweth the way that I take. . . ." You were alone in the desert, and yet you were not alone, for the eyes of God followed your every movement. You were very important, too, for God disturbed a preacher's preparation and transported him from the busy city. At that precise moment, eternal interests were centred in *you*. Probably you have considered this, and have found it to be a source of undying gratitude.

God's Greatness

Now all that we have suggested is proof of the power of God; but the salvation which reached your soul when you trusted Christ, the joy that continued even when your evangelist friend suddenly disappeared, the constant fellowship you enjoyed as you journeyed home to evangelise your own people—these are further indications that what God begins, He is able to conclude. His grace enabled you to discover streams in the desert. His kindness in revealing Christ enabled you to find spiritual realities where only dead formalism had existed. This to us seems to be the background of every true conversion; this is the evidence that what is done in human hearts is all of grace. You agree? Of course you do! One day, we will talk about these things face to face.

The Phenomenal Rise of Social Credit

Dr. T. B. McDormand, the genial and capable General Secretary of the Baptist Federation of Canada, represented his country at the Baptist World Alliance conference held at Ruschlikon, August 2-8, 1958. His stirring address, *Evangelism and a Saving Faith for Modern Man*, seemed to express all that needed to be said concerning this important theme. Dr. McDormand has permitted me to reproduce his closing paragraph. It provides a thrilling illustration of the necessity for, and the possibilities of, *one by one* evangelism.

" In 1934 the Province of Alberta, Canada, witnessed a strange political phenomenon in the rise to power of the so-called Social Credit Party. Totally unknown candidates contended for seats in the legislature, and they represented an unknown and weird economic theory, championed by Major Douglas, of Britain, and espoused in Alberta by a school teacher who was also a lay preacher of extreme premillennial views. No combination of facts should have more completely foredoomed a party to abject defeat at the polls. Yet they won by a large majority, and have held power in Alberta from that day to this. Let me tell you the probable secret of their astonishing success—*Dinner parties in the homes of five thousand Social Credit supporters.*

" Back of this technique was a careful training of leaders —laymen and laywomen; a creative providing of techniques in the form of blackboards and charts; the assignment of a specific number of " parties " to each woman in the ' Social Credit Clubs.' Results followed with the certainty with which Nazism, by actually similar methods, captivated Germany with all its boasted culture and high educational standards; or with which Communism has flourished in certain quarters of the earth through its ' cell ' organisation.

" It seems incredible that the Christian Church, with the supreme ' programme ' as it were, for human life, and with the mightiest organisations and resources ever boasted by any cause in all history, should make so little impact on our present-day society—when we take a really square and un-compromising look at what we are doing. The explanation is to be found to quite a degree in the lack of personal equation in our strategy. We count on church buildings, programmes, educated preachers, large investments of money to produce the results. They never have; they never will; they never can. ' *Ye shall be witnesses unto me* '—that is the divinely appointed strategy; and the Church must mobilise, train, and discipline its witnesses if it is to meet the challenge of this hour. Having trained them, strengthened them in their purpose, it must send them out to bear the good tidings : to the guests in their homes, to the man next door, to sons and daughters, to employers and employees. It must equip them with more effective literature and visual aids. It must learn how to counsel with them concerning their failures, and to rejoice with them in their successes—all within a dynamic fellowship of the concerned, in numbers small and large, organised and spontaneous, in the Church family."

It is problematical whether or not the Christian Church in any one state or county could provide five thousand church members sufficiently enthusiastic to convene dinner parties at which the claims of Christ would be presented to specially invited non-church guests. The Mormon Church sends out missionaries who literally invade non-Mormon communities; the Jehovah Witnesses, in all kinds of weather, stand at street corners endeavouring to place their literature into the hands of the people; Communist agents penetrate deep into the heart of Africa, stirring up trouble among native peoples. All these representatives of an alien faith are keen to spread their teachings, while the rank and file of the Christian community do nothing. Within the circles of the early Church, all members became evangelists; and until we can emulate that inspired example, we cannot even hope to influence the modern world. If every churchman determined to win at least one other soul a year, the world would soon see an upsurge of spiritual power that would dwarf anything known in history.

I was first taught this important fact when I was about fifteen years of age. My pastor had awakened within my heart an interest in winning others for Christ. I quickly found another boy, and to the best of my ability tried to interest him in the church. Later, when opportunity occurred, I spoke to him about the necessity of becoming a Christian, and finally that lad, Clifford Gay, surrendered himself to the Saviour. That same boy, long since grown to manhood, has for many years been a successful missionary from whose lips multitudes have heard the Gospel story. The one-by-one method may produce a harvest of millions!

BARNABAS . . . who loved helping converts

(ACTS 9:27; 11:25)

" And Joses, who by the apostles was surnamed Barnabas (which is, being interpreted, the son of consolation), a Levite, and of the country of Cyprus, having land, sold it, and brought the money, and laid it at the apostles' feet " (Acts 4:36, 37). Splendid! Few men had such a glorious introduction to the sacred record. Barnabas had a great passion —he loved helping people. He was gifted at pouring oil on troubled waters. His soothing words of comfort were to many the balm of Gilead.

The Man and His Virtue

Happy indeed is that man of whom history says, " For he was a good man, full of the Holy Spirit, and of faith . . ." (11:24). When this new member was added to the Church, the fellowship became immeasurably richer. Yet Barnabas never became prominent until the persecutor, Saul of Tarsus, tried to associate with the apostles. He who had easy access to the highest courts in Israel, was barred from the Christian community, because ". . . they were all afraid of him, and believed not that he was a disciple " (9:26). Perhaps the young convert was a little disheartened: " But Barnabas took him, and brought him to the apostles, and declared unto them how he had seen the Lord in the way, and that he had spoken unto him, and how he had preached boldly at Damascus in the name of Jesus " (v. 27). It is easy to imagine that when Barnabas heard of Saul's embarrassment, he sought him, sat with him to hear his story, and then pouring consolation into the wounded soul of the young man, took him to the leaders of the Church. Well done, Barnabas! You were a genius!

The Man and His Vision

Probably they became friends, and Barnabas was a little sad when Saul was sent home to Tarsus (v. 30). However, the convert was in danger, and " prevention was better than cure." There is reason to believe they never saw each other for three years (Gal. 1:18). During all this time, Saul was being instructed by God in what he afterward called " my Gospel." Then came the revival in Antioch, necessitating help from the parent Church. Young people needed guidance, persecuted converts needed comfort; and when these facts were brought before the apostles, ". . . they sent forth Barnabas, that he should go as far as Antioch. Who, when he came, and had seen the grace of God, was glad, and exhorted them all, that with purpose of heart they should cleave unto the Lord" (11:22, 23). Surrounded by these young Christians, and probably feeling unequal to the demands being made upon him, Barnabas thought of his friend Saul of Tarsus. "Then departed Barnabas to Tarsus, for to seek Saul. And when he had found him, he brought him unto Antioch . . . (vv. 25, 26). Barnabas was never as good a speaker as Saul (14:12) but his influence on the man of fire was invaluable. Truly he was "the son of consolation," and his untiring companionship increased immeasurably the power of his friend's ministry. And while Barnabas helped the one convert, he cherished ambitions of finding another of his type; so after a little discussion, "Barnabas and Saul . . . took with them John, whose surname was Mark" (12.25). Well done, Barnabas.

The Man and His Vacillation

Alas, John Mark failed, and thereafter storm clouds loomed in the sky of the two missionary pioneers. At a later stage they quarrelled, "And the contention was so sharp between them, that they departed asunder one from the other: and so Barnabas took Mark, and sailed unto Cyprus; and Paul chose Silas, and departed, being recommended by the brethren unto the grace of God" (15:39-40). It would be easy to blame this unfortunate quarrel on the unrelenting Paul; but this was only the climax of something which had been going on for months. Poor Barnabas had been slipping. Even Peter momentarily lapsed when arrogant Jewish teachers proclaimed the supremacy of the law. The church had been divided; and following Peter's example " . . . the other Jews dissembled likewise with him; insomuch that Barnabas also was carried away with their dissimulation" (Gal. 2:11-13). Coming events cast their shadows before. Barnabas, alas, had taken his eyes from the Master. But at least Barnabas was consistent. He came into the Bible story helping a young convert called Saul; he went out of the same story trying to help another young convert called John Mark. Happy is the man who lives to help others. See *Bible Treasures*, 129; *Bible Cameos*, 157.

The Tent Hall, Glasgow, was packed with over two thousand people, and their enthusiastic singing rang through the famous old building as they waited for the " Saturday at Seven " meeting to begin. Soon, I would be required to preach again, and sitting quietly in the superintendent's room, I prepared for the moment when I would stand before the large audience. Then the door slowly opened and an usher said, " Mr. Powell, here is a brother who wants to see you." He stood aside to permit the entry of a negro. The visitor seemed shy; I think he was a little conscious of his colour, for the room was filled with Europeans. He was very smart, but apparently nervous as he looked for "the man from Wales." His collar silently announced the fact that he had been ordained to preach the Gospel. Suddenly he saw me, and immediately his face beamed. " Ah, Mr. Powell, it is wonderful to see you. Do you remember me?" I smiled and admitted that I could not recollect ever having met him. I blamed my poor memory, and admitted that I should have known him instantly: but perhaps I was getting old! " Mr. Powell, do you remember coming to preach at a Sunday evening service in British Honduras House in Edinburgh?" I stared—it was quite impossible. " Ah, sir, you *do* remember. I can see you do. Mr Powell, I was one of those whom you led to the Saviour."

Fourteen years earlier, I had accepted the invitation of the Rev. David Laurie to conduct a crusade in Carrubber's Close Mission, Edinburgh, and it was at the close of one of the meetings that a married couple came forward to ask a favour. " Sir, we know you are very busy, but we are wondering if you can help us. We are trying so hard to hold meetings in British Honduras House, but sometimes we get discouraged. Mr. Powell, the building has been set aside for the use of the coloured soldiers, but the place is overrun by prostitutes. To go into the place is like going into hell! They do not really want us; they merely tolerate us because of certain amenities which come their way. We have a service each Sunday evening, and we would love you to come and speak to these young people."

I looked at my audience, and discarded my prepared sermon. This was no place for homiletics. The soldiers were tall, and extremely tough. The white girls did not enhance the virtues of their sex. During the opening hymns the audience giggled; the girls were playing up to their overseas friends, the boys were rolling their big eyes. The man whose invitation I had accepted, announced that a visitor had come to address the meeting, and instantly all eyes were focused on me. I have long since forgotten the details of that strange address; I know only that I spoke of sin, of the evil consequences of forgetting God, and of the joy I found when I surrendered my life to Christ. At first it was extremely difficult to interest the listeners, but after a while even the unfortunate girls became respectful. When I gave the invitation to yield to the Lord Jesus, several of the soldiers responded, and with them came one young lady whose speech suggested she belonged to a good home. I explained how they could become Christians, and then returned to the manse in which I was staying.

" Yes, sir, I was one of those whom you led to Jesus. The gentleman and his wife held on to me, and taught me many things about the Bible. I grew in grace, and eventually was able to go to the divinity school. Quite recently I graduated and was ordained, and in August I am returning to British Honduras to become a missionary to my own people. When I heard you were coming to Glasgow I was so happy, because I wanted to see once again the man who led me to Christ."

" It's seven o'clock, Mr. Powell. It's time to be on our way." When I gripped my brother's hand and whispered, " God bless you," my heart was full. Then two elderly people came forward to say, " Mr. Powell, we would like to shake hands also." I hardly knew what to say, for these were the wonderful couple who had invited me to speak at the memorable meeting. They were very much like Barnabas of old, for they found their greatest happiness in helping converts. I have since wondered what would have happened to the negro Christian if they had failed to do their duty.

CORNELIUS . . . who received a strange warning

Cornelius was the most revered elder of his church, and chairman of most of its committees. Each Sabbath he bowed in the sacred house, and each weekday he lived a life worthy of his noblest generosity; a target for every needy society. A man of integrity, he adorned his town, was an important member of the council, and a very desirable friend. A person of bearing, breeding, culture, he was known and regarded by the highest officials in the nation, and his name was often mentioned in the society columns of the newspapers. He was certain of election to parliament, but—reader, let me apologise. My mistake is inexcusable, my tenses have been confused. I should have said that Cornelius would have become such a man if he had belonged to a later generation.

He was Good—but He was not Saved

"There was a certain man in Caesarea called Cornelius . . . a devout man, and one that feared God with all his house, which gave much alms to the people, and prayed to God always" (Acts 10:1, 2). Cornelius was the kind of man who regularly studied the Scriptures, and daily presided at morning and evening family prayers. His sincerity was indisputable, and his influence extended throughout the town. He had few equals: yet in the sight of God he was unsaved. He was certainly good according to moral standards, but he was not a Christian. When his servants interviewed Simon Peter, they affirmed that their master had been *warned* by God to send for help. And when, later, Peter explained his conduct to the apostles, he stated that God had declared, " Peter shall tell thee words whereby thou and all thy house *shall be saved* " (11:14). Obviously, then, good works plus a sincere religious belief are not sufficient to guarantee a man's salvation.

He was Wise—so He did not argue

There are many people in this world who are the exact replica of Cornelius, except for one important detail. Whereas the man of old listened quietly to the suggestions of God's Spirit, his modern counterparts love to argue. Humility is the child of sincerity, and Cornelius was never seen to better advantage than when he bowed before God and His servant to hear the way of salvation. The fact that God *warned* this great man was truly suggestive. This was not advice; it was not merely instruction. Warning implies danger. The love of God embraced the entire world, but a man whose integrity equalled that of Cornelius attracted great attention. His very attitude demanded that God should bring to him the light of additional knowledge.

He was Anxious—so He did not Procrastinate

" And when the angel which spake unto Cornelius was departed, he called two of his household servants, and a devout soldier of them that waited on him continually; and when he had declared all these things unto them, he sent them to Joppa " (10:7, 8). If a warning revealed danger, then danger demanded action. This was a matter of paramount importance needing urgent attention. Other people might have decided to give the affair prolonged consideration; some might have shrugged their shoulders, dismissing this as an empty vision. Some might have even shared their thoughts with fellow men, and as a result would have been talked out of their intentions. Cornelius was a wise man. His sincere endeavours had failed to produce satisfaction. His piety had only increased his desire for improvement, and as soon as the voice of God reached his ears, he immediately took steps to obey the new commandments. His glorious example might well serve as our guiding star. Tomorrow is the most uncertain thing in the calendar.

He Believed—and He was not Ashamed

" The path of the just is as a shining light, which shineth more and more unto the perfect day " (Prov. 4:18). When God revealed His acceptance of this Gentile soldier and his company, Peter marvelled and said, " Can any man forbid water, that these should not be baptised . . . And he commanded them to be baptised in the name of the Lord. Then prayed they him to tarry certain days " (Acts 10:47, 48). Cornelius was an officer in the Italian army of occupation. His baptism would invite attention in many places, and since Christianity was considered to be an enemy of the State, serious repercussions could follow. Cornelius smiled and went ahead with his plans. He had found a new life, and was not ashamed.

The Bishop's Sermon

Years ago, during city-wide services in Glasgow, Scotland, I stayed with six other ministers in a central hotel, and among our number was the Rev. Chalmers Lyons, a forthright preacher of the Gospel. I shall always remember a story he told of his travels in Germany. Accompanied by Bishop

Taylor Smith, he was going from place to place; and one Saturday evening the Bishop looked at his friend and said, " Lyons, I'll give you a sermon for tomorrow."

" Yes, Bishop; what is the text?"

" Lord, by this time he stinketh."

" But, Bishop, I can hardly speak from that text."

" Why not? I used it in an English cathedral only a few months ago. I had a great time with it."

Chalmers Lyons stared at the Bishop; it seemed inconceivable that such a text could provide subject matter for an address in a dignified cathedral. Then, as he recognised that the Bishop was not leg-pulling, he continued, " Bishop, you preached from that text: what did you say about it?"

" Well, I had three points: (i) A dead body cannot save itself; (ii) A dead body only deteriorates—it gets worse and worse; (iii) Christ alone can do anything in the matter."

Chalmers Lyons paused, and his eyes were twinkling. " You must admit,". he added, " the old Bishop had some excellent thoughts there, and I told him so." Then he continued, " But the Bishop had not completed his story. He went on to say, ' Lyons, after the service had ended, I went to the vestry to disrobe, and was surprised when the Dean of the cathedral followed me in and locked the door.' ' Bishop,' said the Dean, ' your text upset me greatly.' ' Well,' responded the Bishop, ' it was true, was it not?' ' Yes, that is what I mean. You stressed the fact that men dead in sins cannot save themselves; they grow worse and worse. You said that even the finest body ultimately dies; that the coming of Christ in resurrection power is essential. All men need to be born again. Bishop, it is true, but I never knew it until tonight. I need that new life.' "

And there, behind a locked door, they knelt to pray, and that scholarly man entered into newness of life. The Bishop concluded his story by saying, " I heard from him a little while ago. He is rejoicing, but some of his colleagues cannot understand what has happened to him. He is so different! So there you are, Lyons; the text is an excellent one. Use it tomorrow." And smiling broadly, the Bishop went his way.

Paul and His Faulty Grammar

Sometimes when I preach the Gospel, I refer to Paul's text, " Unto me, who am less than the least of all saints, is this grace given, that I should preach among the Gentiles the unsearchable riches of Christ " (Ephes. 3 : 8). This utterance always takes me back in thought to the High School in Wales where, years ago, I had a most formidable English mistress. With untiring persistence she instilled into the minds of her scholars the principles of English grammar, and it was no cause for amazement when she became increasingly unpopular. I have often said that I would love to listen to a debate between my old teacher and the apostle Paul. Undoubtedly she would reprove him for the loose way in which he handled superlatives; perhaps he would retaliate by telling her she had much to learn! " Unto me, who am *less than the least* . . . " It is not possible to be less than the least. No man can be lower than the lowest, for if he be lower than the lowest, then the lowest is *not* the lowest—*he* is the lowest!

At least, that is what my old teacher would have said. This text is the last of three which I like to quote. Here is progression of thought. At the beginning of his ministry Paul declared, " Paul, an apostle by the will of God." When he was much older he added, " Unto me, who am less than the least of all saints . . . " Finally, in writing to Timothy, he reached a glorious climax when he said, " This is a faithful saying, and worthy of all acceptation, that Christ Jesus came into the world to save sinners; *of whom I am chief* " (1 Tim. 1:15). Paul's wisdom increased with his age. (i) An apostle; (ii) The lowest saint; (iii) The greatest sinner. The closer one gets to the light, the more easily one sees the dirt. Cornelius, Paul, Nicodemas, and a host of others would corroborate this statement. We are not saved by works, lest any man should boast. Eternal life is the *gift* of God: but it is only given to those who know their need; to those who come humbly, seeking from God's hand that which could never be received in any other way.

FAITH AND CONFESSION . . . the Siamese twins of Scripture

(ROMANS 10:9, 10)

These verses are among the best-known Bible texts. Here the heart of the Gospel is presented; here one meets the Siamese twins of Holy Writ. Faith and confession belong to each other. To separate them is to run the risk of losing them. If faith brings eternal life, confession brings joy. If faith opens the door of a man's soul, confession invites the Saviour to enter. When certain Bible stories are brought together, the composite picture becomes most illuminating. The purpose of this study is to compare and contrast lessons which have already found individual places in *Bible Pinnacles* and *Bible Treasures*.

A Captain Condemned

The scene was resplendent yet strangely bewildering. The Syrians were eager, excited, thrilled. Their master, the famous Naaman, had been cleansed of his leprosy. They had seen what humanly speaking was impossible. A miracle had been performed before their eyes. Naaman was a man in a dream! His anger had gone. Clothed with the garments of humility, he returned thanks and commenced his homeward journey. A new faith filled his soul; the eternal God had become his Saviour. His return to Syria was hailed with delight; but soon the priests of Rimmon were proclaiming far and wide that their god had answered their prayers. The increasing fervour of the crowds reached a climax when the temple was packed with excited worshippers. Rimmon, sombre, silent, still, seemed to look down on the specially convened thanksgiving service, and even the king was grateful as he stood before the high altar. Naaman, in pensive mood, also was present. The voice of the presiding priest was animated: " People, our great god Rimmon has performed a miracle. Before us stands Naaman. He was a leper; he was in danger of death. Look at him now, and return thanks to our god." A glad cry echoed through the temple as the entire audience bowed before the sightless idol. When Naaman bowed, he ruined for ever his chance of becoming God's messenger to Syria. He believed in his heart (2 Kings 5:15), but he never confessed with his mouth (v. 18). And although the prophet gave the customary farewell blessing, his heart surely grieved that a man who had received so much, should be content to return so little.

A Parent Petrified

The street was filled with arguing people; the situation was almost out of control. Demonstrators were waving their arms, voices were unnecessarily loud. A buzz of excitement at the corner of the street announced the arrival of the ecclesiastical leaders. They were obviously annoyed. This situation was outrageous! Had the people forgotten the sanctity of the Sabbath? Even the healing of a blind man was no excuse for undignified conduct. Of course it was all stupidity. They would settle the matter at once. " Woman, are you the mother of this fellow? And is that your husband? Then tell these fools they are mistaken. They have allowed themselves to become bewitched. Tell them this is not your blind son, or explain ' how then doth he now see.' " " His parents answered them and said, We know that this is our son, and that he was born blind: but by what means he now seeth, we know not, or who hath opened his eyes, we know not: he is of age, ask him; he shall speak for himself. *These words spake his parents because they feared the Jews* . . . " (John 9: 18-22). The doorway of their home might have become a pulpit that day; they might have been prophets indeed! Their faith was stifled by fear.

A Disciple Determined

Peter's conscience was aflame. He would remember eternally the night of shame when he had failed his Master. Grim lines of determination were now upon his face as he stood before the crowd. He knew this was one way to atone for his former failure. " Ye men of Judaea," he cried, " know assuredly, that God hath made that same Jesus, whom ye have crucified, both Lord and Christ " (Acts 2:14 & 36). The epic story of Peter's preaching makes good reading. In retrospect, we rejoice as we see thousands of people responding to the new message. Yet we do well to consider that when the other disciples stood up with their preacher, they were unaware of the success to attend his efforts. Earlier the crowd had crucified the Lord; later that same crowd would consent to the stoning of Stephen. Yet, unafraid and unashamed, the eleven stood with Peter during that memorable meeting, and when the flood-tides of Pentecostal blessing brought thousands of souls into the kingdom of God, the men who had probably expected stones, grasped the chance of leading people to Christ. Their faith was wedded to confession, and it is written that great grace and much joy was among them all.

Please Can You Sell Me a Miracle?

J. B. Gough, in telling the following story, assured his listeners he was able to vouch for its truthfulness. A small child living with her family in one of the poorest quarters of a large city, heard the doctor saying that only a miracle could save her sick sister. Taking the pennies from her money box, she began a tour of the shops asking if they were able to sell her a miracle. Puzzled, the tradesmen told her that they did not sell miracles; but undaunted, the child continued her search, and coming to a chemist's shop made her request. Another gentleman heard her, and asked why she desired to purchase a miracle. He was a famous surgeon, and hearing the child's story accompanied her to the bedside of her sister. After examining the patient, he agreed that a miracle was needed, but added that this may be possible. He made the necessary arrangements for the child to be taken into hospital, and performed the operation himself. The child recovered. She owed her life to the doctor's skill and the believing petition of her small sister.

During an evangelistic crusade in Grahamstown, South Africa, several student teachers professed faith in Christ. I shall always remember one of the number. She was a fine young lady, who came forward at the end of a service, trusted Christ, and then went away radiantly happy. Yet when she attended the next meeting, I saw from the pulpit that she seemed intensely miserable. This continued for a week, and each night her gloom appeared to have deepened. To say the least I was very disappointed, and wondered what had happened to spoil the convert's happiness. Then one night she came into the church supremely happy, and again I wondered what had taken place. Immediately the service had concluded the young lady came into the vestry to tell her story.

" Mr. Powell, I was so happy when you introduced me to the Lord Jesus; but when I returned to the college, to the dormitory where several students sleep, I became afraid of one student teacher. She was always a bully, and I thought she would sneer if she discovered I had become a Christian. I slid my Bible into the locker, and said my prayers in bed! I knew this was wrong, but I feared that girl. Then last night, things came to a climax. I had just returned from the meeting and was about to put my Bible away, when she came down to my bed and loudly asked, ' What is this I hear about you?' I answered, ' What do you mean?' and immediately she announced for all to hear, that I had become a Christian, and had gone forward during one of your meetings in the city. ' Why didn't you tell us?' she demanded. Mr. Powell, I knew it was then or never, and confessed I had been afraid of her reactions. Oh, sir, she just lifted her hand and thumped me on the back, and then said, 'You little fool, if I had any courage I would have become a Christian long ago. Kid, that is the best thing you will ever do.' Then she turned to the other girls and said, 'Listen, you lot. This kid has given her life to Christ. If I see any of you throwing a slipper when she kneels to pray, or if I hear any sneering at her, you will have me to deal with.' Mr. Powell, for a whole week I have been scared of her, but now she is my greatest champion. Oh, sir, I am so happy." This story perfectly illustrates the truths of Romans 10:9. Faith without confession is hardly *faith*.

On the eve of D-Day in World War II, a young sailor came into my services in Exmouth, Devonshire, England. After surrendering his life to Christ, he returned to the hotel in which, with many others, he had been billeted. His comrades were amazed when unashamedly he confessed what he had done. While he was speaking a stranger entered. Actually the newcomer was a Christian who had been in the navy many years. Not knowing the new man was a fellow Christian, the convert said, " Yes, and you are just in time to hear it also," and the testimony was repeated. When the boy finished, the older man shook his hand and said, " Son, I trusted Christ years ago—aye, before you were born. That is the best thing you will ever do." Then from the rear of the long room came a tall thin recruit who faced the audience and said, " This kid makes me ashamed. Before I joined up I always went to church. Yes, I was a Christian; but when I met you lot, I had no backbone. I drank and gambled with you, but all the while I felt ashamed and condemned. Now this boy speaks about his faith in Christ and makes me feel a worm. Fellow, let me shake your hand. You have courage."

In those moments the young convert discovered the truth— the twin truths—of Romans 10:9. Faith and confession are indeed the Siamese twins of Holy Scripture.

CHRIST . . . and the size of our bank balance

(EPHESIANS 1-3)

Paul would have made an excellent bank manager! He possessed an expert knowledge of sound investments. There are great financiers who, in spite of increasing wealth, are too poor to purchase a moment of happiness; there are ordinary labourers who possess the heavens. Wealth is a peculiar thing: sometimes in filling the hand it empties the heart. Paul's exposition of eternal wealth falls into four sections, but the connecting link is Christ.

In Whom we have redemption—1:7

It must be remembered that in ancient times redemption was something vitally linked with slavery. If a man were beset by adverse circumstances, he could sell himself and become a slave. A friend might endeavour to obtain his release, but if the slave owner insisted, the man remained in bondage. The only exception to this rule was made in the case of a kinsman (Lev. 25:48). Any person belonging to the slave's family could pay the redemption money and demand the liberation of the unfortunate kinsman. Paul saw in the bondage of sin a slavery destined to chain the soul for ever. Then the Son of God became bone of our bone and flesh of our flesh. Through the miracle of Bethlehem Christ became our kinsman; through the triumph of the Cross the debt was paid. In Him we have redemption—we go out *free*.

In Whom we have an inheritance—1:11

Here we have progression in Paul's thinking. Redemption set free the slave, but the liberated man could be poor and in extreme need. The news that the freed man is suddenly to receive a great inheritance is truly astounding. Redemption means liberty; an inheritance suggests wealth. Nevertheless an inheritance must be claimed, and certain formalities observed. The person from whom the money is to come might have made certain conditions, and the man to benefit needs to acquaint himself with these details. " . . . being predestinated according to the purpose of him who worketh all things after the counsel of his own will: that we should be to the praise of his glory " (1:11, 12). " For whom he did foreknow, he also did predestinate *to be conformed to the image of his Son* . . . " (Rom. 8:29). Eternal wealth thus comes within our grasp; but conformity to the divine pattern is requisite. For this purpose we are sealed with the Holy Spirit —we are God's possession.

In Whom ye are builded together for an habitation of God—
   2:22

The church of God knows no racial barriers, "for he is our peace, who hath made Jew and Gentile one, and hath broken down the middle wall of partition between us" (2:14). There are many slaves who have found new freedom. Their gratitude knows no limitation, for they desire to become the perpetual servants of their new Master. The Old Testament slaves who preferred to remain slaves had holes bored in their ears: this was the sign of their willingness to stay servants for ever (Deut. 15:16, 17). Similarly God's sign is placed on our hearts when the Holy Spirit comes to take control. The Christian who avoids fellowship advertises the sickness of his soul. The church of God is the greatest institution in existence, for within its circle fellowship banishes loneliness, the bread of life removes soul-hunger, and God draws near to His people.

In Whom we have boldness and access unto the Father—
   2:18; 3:12

Every true Christian is well acquainted with the path of prayer. *Boldness* brings one to the royal door; *access* reveals that the door is open. Redemption replaces rags with the garments of salvation; the inheritance replaces fear with a sure hope for the future; the fellowship banishes loneliness, and introduces one to the greatest happiness in the world; access to God opens the divine treasure house and supplies an open cheque on eternal riches (see 3:16-19). There is no one quite as wealthy as the man who walks with God. To be filled with the fullness of God is to be a millionaire. Thus Paul covers the entire range of redemptive truth. The Cross liberates us; the risen Christ supplies an inheritance; Pentecost brings the Holy Spirit to unite the redeemed slaves; the High Priestly work of the Saviour makes access to God a reality. Ephesians 2:4, 5 reveals the riches of the past; v. 6 reminds of the riches of the present; v. 7 surpasses all, and reveals the unspeakable joy of the future. The epistle to the Ephesians is indeed a guide for wise and ambitious investments. It is possible to invest time as well as money, and the dividends are excellent! This is a gilt-edged security!

He Managed a Bottle Store

I first saw him when he arose from his seat in a crowded Sunday evening evangelistic service in South Africa. His appearance commanded attention. He was tall and stately, his hair was silvery grey; but worry had lined his face. He was the manager of a bottle store! He desired to become a

Christian, but was unwilling to leave his employment. One year later I returned to his city, and found him waiting to speak to me. He was desperate, and confessed he had been planning to commit suicide. I reminded him of my earlier words, and reaffirmed that happiness would be quite impossible unless he ceased meddling with liquor. He refused to consider the idea, so I promised to send a wreath to his funeral. "What do you mean?" he asked. "Well," I replied, "the way you are going on, you will soon be in your coffin, and a few flowers might help to brighten the procession." Within a few days the slave was free; and then came the news of his "inheritance." Although he was advanced in age, new employment was quickly forthcoming, and ultimately he was able to consider the purchase of his house. When the owner heard his testimony, she asked how long he had been her tenant and how much rent per month she had received. Then she astounded him by saying, "You can purchase the house, and all the money I have received as rent shall be considered as payment on the price of the house." Her announcement left him speechless, for it meant he was to get the house for practically nothing!

Stamping Canadian Logs

I shall never forget my first train journey in Canada. My wife and I had disembarked at Quebec, but since the first preaching appointment was to be in the Acadia University in Wolfville, it was necessary to journey into the Maritime Provinces. I sat at the compartment window watching the huge rivers in which millions of logs were floating toward the waiting mills. Canadian logging companies purchase vast areas of timber, and when the logs are ready for delivery each one is stamped or sealed with the company's mark. Then they are slipped into the surging waters, and the journey down-stream begins. Before this is completed the logs mingle with many others; but the sealing mark is indelible. When the time comes to lift the logs from the water, identity of ownership is never in doubt. Similarly, Christ purchased us with His own blood, and *we are sealed with the Holy Spirit.* In our journey through time, we may be among millions of other human logs, but God's seal in our hearts is never removed. When the great day of complete and ultimate redemption dawns, we shall be lifted from the river of time to take our place in His great plans for eternity.

He Can Get Me In!

The story has often been told of a little boy who looked through the railings guarding Buckingham Palace. His face reflected the desires of his heart, when Prince Edward saw him. Taking the lad by the hand, the Prince conducted him through the great gate and into the royal apartments. When Queen Victoria heard of the boy's interest, she commanded that he should be washed and clothed with a new suit, and when finally she sent him forth, he seemed a prince in his own right. I remember a night in New Zealand when a young woman found difficulty in understanding how she could be accepted by God. At that time the present Queen and her husband were touring the land, and I reminded my listener that the royal visitors were staying in Government House. She agreed that this was so, and that the place was well guarded by officials and soldiers. I asked, " What would happen to you if you tried to get in through the back window to see the Queen?" Her answer was rather explosive when she said, " I should be out on my neck!" " But supposing the Duke of Edinburgh came out to say, ' So you desire to see the Queen, and cannot. Young lady, do not worry, just come with me and I will take you to her.' What would happen then?" " He could get me in." She understood when I said, " We would never gain admittance into the Royal House of Heaven. Our sins would keep us out. Yet the Prince of Peace came forth to seek us, and His word is, ' I am the way, the truth, and the life; no man cometh unto the Father, but by me.' " Perhaps the apostle Paul had such thoughts in his mind when he wrote, " In whom we have boldness and access unto the Father." The Lord Jesus brings to us redemption, an inheritance, security, and the inestimable privilege of communing with our heavenly Father. Christ is the secret of all true wealth. He is the key to the divine treasure house; He supplies it all.

A GREAT INHERITANCE . . . for us and for Christ

(EPHESIANS 1:11-18)

I shall always remember the old lady who decided to bequeath to me her fortune. " My boy," she said, " I am a wealthy woman. I have property in England and South Africa, but I cannot expect to live much longer. I have decided to leave my possessions to you." When she smiled, she seemed an angel! Thereafter I walked on air until one of the local people asked how I was getting along with my hostess. Possibly he saw the excitement in my eyes, for he said, " She is a wonderful old lady, but she has one weakness. Has she spoken about her will yet? She makes one every month, and probably gets a real kick out of doing it. Has she told you she intends to leave everything to you? Ah, I thought so. She is always approaching new people with the same story. Her lawyer must be a patient man." Yes, that kindly lady made me her sole beneficiary, but she forgot to die—in time. " For where a testament is, there must also of necessity be the death of the testator. For a testament is of force *after* men are dead; otherwise it is of no strength at all while the testator liveth " (Heb. 9:16, 17). An inheritance depends upon three things: (i) Someone must have something to bequeath; (ii) That person must die before the will becomes operative; (iii) Then the beneficiary can claim the inheritance and rejoice in its provision.

Our Inheritance in Christ—1-11

Paul speaks of our inheritance in Christ, and then affirms that the Lord Jesus also has an inheritance in us. The Saviour had something to bequeath, and His death made it possible for beneficiaries to register claims. Against the background of slavery, the apostle speaks of redemption through the blood of Christ; but in Ephesians 2:5-7 the magnificent sweep of his vision encompasses the eternal breadth of God's purposes for the church. In the past, He quickened us together with Christ; in the present, He has made us to sit in the place of divine power; in the future, He intends to display His eternal kindness before the assembled hosts of heaven. When Royalty honours a subject, the act is reported around the world. Similarly, ". . . in the ages to come he might show the exceeding riches of his grace in his kindness toward us through Jesus Christ." The forgiveness of sins, eternal life, the filling of the Holy Spirit, enduement of power, and the assurance that some day we shall be like Him, are all part of our great inheritance. Sometimes earthly inheritances are conditioned by restrictive clauses; a man may not register his claim until he has reached a specified age. Our inheritance may be claimed *now*.

Christ's Inheritance in Us—1 : 18

It should be noted that, while Paul rejoiced in the first inheritance, he prayed for wisdom to grasp the full significance of the second. He prayed for three things: (i) That Christians might understand the purpose of God's call—the *hope* of His calling. There were things for which Christ fervently hoped. The apostle spoke of an *inheritance*. He envisaged the joys of ownership, and thought not only of a soul forgiven but of one possessed. An inheritance possessed may be used by its recipient to further his purposes and increase his pleasure. Christ plans to reach a world, but to do so needs instruments. Second only to the joy of possessing men is the thrill of using them. There is much latent wealth in the human soul, and this may be bequeathed to the Saviour. Yet in spite of every noble resolve, the fulfilment of our will can never be accomplished until we also die—" for a testament is of force after men are dead." We need to be crucified with Christ, for only then can the Lord Jesus take His inheritance. Thus (ii) Paul prays that Christians may become conversant with the details of this great inheritance; and (iii) asks that men might know " . . . the exceeding greatness of his power to usward who believe . . . " Yet the key to all this is the crucifixion of the self-life. The cross of Calvary stands at the centre of everything spiritual. Through His death for us we may inherit the riches of heaven; through our death for Him, He can inherit the riches of earth. He was glad to lay down His life for us; it is problematical whether we shall be glad to emulate His example. Elsewhere Paul speaks of our being labourers together with God—we are partners in a great concern. Together we work toward the one great end. However, we do well to consider a question. We have been able to claim our inheritance; has He been able to claim His?

> Oh, teach me how to die, dear Lord;
>   To die upon a cross:
> To give to Thee that which is Thine,
>   And count all else but dross.
> Then teach me how to live, dear Lord,
>   To take Thy hand in mine:
> To work, and pray, and seek for souls,
>   Until the world is Thine.

162

The Slave Who Refused His Freedom

Perhaps the supreme illustration of this two-way inheritance comes from the Bible itself. Under Mosaic law, provision was made whereby a slave could refuse his freedom in order to continue in the service of his master. In Exodus 21:2-6 we read the following commandment: " If thou buy an Hebrew servant, six years he shall serve: and in the seventh he shall go out free for nothing. If he came in by himself he shall go out by himself: if he were married, then his wife shall go out with him. If his master have given him a wife, and she have borne him sons or daughters; the wife and her children shall be her master's and he shall go out by himself. And if the servant shall plainly say, I love my master, my wife, and my children; I will not go out free: then his master shall bring him unto the judges; he shall also bring him to the door, or unto the doorpost; and his master shall bore his ear through with an aul; and he shall serve him for ever." Here is clearly defined the difference between bondage and dedicated service. A slave may serve because he has no alternative. When he rejects freedom because love prompts further service, the Master may be assured this servant will be worth his weight in gold! The Master's kindness begets increasing love.

To be free is the greatest heritage of all, yet when a man voluntarily chooses to remain a slave—when he puts to death the inherent longings of his soul—the life which follows will be completely dedicated. The master thereupon inherits in his servant a wealth of devotion and service hitherto unknown.

> I love, I love my Master,
> I will not go out free:
> For He is my Redeemer,
> He paid the price for me.

Why Don't You Get Out of the Way?

It is problematical whether Wales ever produced a greater preacher than the late Rev. R. B. Jones, for the influence of this man of God reached every part of the Principality. His untiring activity, his soul-stirring oratory, his deep faith in the Word of God, were those of a true prophet. All his students revered him, and to sit at his feet was unforgettable. Years after I had left his lecture hall, I stayed in the home of a saintly lady who had known the beloved Principal for many years. She told me of earlier times, when as a young minister R. B. Jones had first made an impact upon the Christian church. He was young, eloquent, determined, dominant. Everywhere he went, congregations overflowed the churches; yet something seemed to be lacking. Then one day a certain woman, a close friend of the young minister, said to him, " Why don't *you* get out of the way?" It was enough. From that moment God filled the soul of His servant with new power, and I am only one of the very many people who will forever thank God for the privilege of meeting and knowing this great man.

Dr. Scroggie's Testimony

I once heard Dr. Graham Scroggie tell a Keswick audience that he could remember a time in his early years in the ministry when he reached the end of himself. He was convinced he was a failure, and would never succeed in the ministry. Then one day he climbed a hillside, and sat in the shadow of a tree. Around him the world seemed to be falling to pieces; the outlook was bleak indeed. " And then," said Dr. Scroggie, " He took me, and blessed me, and brake me; and ever since has used me to feed a hungry multitude." Silently the great Keswick audience listened to the speaker as he developed his point. The greatest thing a Christian can do is to die; to reach that place of self abnegation where he is able to say, " I am crucified with Christ: nevertheless I live; yet not I, but Christ liveth in me: and the life which I now live in the flesh, I live by the faith of the Son of God, who loved me, and gave himself for me " (Gal. 2: 20). Dr. Scroggie had received a great inheritance through the death of his Redeemer; the Lord Jesus received a similar inheritance when beneath a hillside tree His weary servant gave up depending upon self-sufficiency.

It has been said that John Newton was once the slave of a slave woman; that he had reached depths of human depravity unknown by most civilised people. Then Christ found him, and the grace of God commenced to lift the fallen man from the depths of shame. Gradually John Newton became stronger in the Christian faith, and ultimately entered the ministry. His charm and power as a saintly preacher were recognised in high circles, and finally the former slave of a slave woman became the rector of a renowned church in the City of London. This was the man who wrote—

> How sweet the name of Jesus sounds
>   In a believer's ear;
> It soothes his sorrows, heals his wounds,
>   And drives away his fear.

PAUL ... and his superb bankruptcy

(PHILIPPIANS 3:8-9)

From time immemorial, the Christian life has been likened to a journey on which the saint has had to fight his way onward. Perhaps Israel's march to Canaan originally inspired this idea, but Paul in writing the Epistle to the Ephesians certainly had similar thoughts in mind. He said that Christians would need the whole armour of God, for only thus would they be able to stand against the wiles of the devil. The apostle John also wrote, " This is the victory that overcometh the world, our faith (1 John 5:4). *This is the means whereby we triumph—our faith.* We are indebted to John for this remarkable verse, but Paul is the ideal exponent of the truth.

Righteousness by Faith

Paul was one of the noblest characters in the ancient world. Some preachers have permitted his persecution of the early church to blind them with prejudice, but it must be remembered that Paul's fierce onslaught upon the new faith was governed by the fact that he considered this upstart sect to be a menace to the cause of God; the Carpenter to be an irresponsible deceiver. A true gauge of the quality of his morality may be found in his testimony, ". . . touching the righteousness which is in the law, I was blameless." Paul was an excellent man prior to his conversion, but afterward he reached heights never before known. Of his Christian conduct he said, " And herein do I exercise myself, to have always a conscience void of offence toward God, and toward men " (Acts 24:16). Of all men he might have boasted most concerning his virtue, yet he pronounced himself to be a bankrupt. Believing his own righteousness to be utterly insufficient, he said, " Yea doubtless, and I count all things but loss . . . that I may be found in Christ, not having mine own righteousness, which is of the law, but that which is through the faith of Christ, the righteousness which is of God by faith." If such an exemplary character needed a righteousness other than his own, I am quite sure that I need it.

Reassurance by Faith

The ship was going down. Overcome by worry and excessive duties, the crew were exhausted; their immediate future was bleak. Describing those awful days, Luke wrote, " And when neither sun nor stars in many days appeared, and no small tempest lay on us, all hope that we should be saved was then taken away" (Acts 27:20). Every sailor was anxious, and some were frantic; yet down in his small cabin Paul was completely calm. He was in good company, for the radiance of an angel had illuminated both his cabin and his soul. Later, when he stood before the bewildered sailors, his voice throbbed with confidence as he said, ". . . There stood by me this night the angel of God, whose I am and whom I serve, saying, Fear not Paul; thou must be brought before Caesar, and lo, God hath given thee all them that sail with thee. Wherefore, sirs, be of good cheer: for I believe God, that it shall be even as it was told me" (vv. 23-25). Faith brought Paul to the heavenly pathway; faith strengthened him as he progressed along it. My surrender to the Saviour does not imply that trials and tribulations will never be encountered again. God never promised to remove my difficulties, but rather I should never be expected to face them alone.

Resplendent by Faith

Paul, old before his time, sat in his unlovely prison; thoughts were his only companions. Sometimes the beloved Doctor Luke was allowed to visit his old friend, but apart from the famous physician, few men even thought of the prisoner. Sitting alone, Paul became reminiscent, and taking his pen, wrote to Timothy. "I am now ready to be offered, and the time of my departure is at hand. I have fought a good fight, I have finished my course, I have kept the faith: henceforth there is laid up for me a crown of righteousness, which the Lord, the righteous judge, shall give me . . . " (2 Tim. 4:6, 7). Paul might easily have said, "Henceforth there is laid up for me a coffin—a sepulchre—a martyr's death." No. Faith had saved him; faith had strengthened him; faith would now succour him in his hour of need. Faith would make this the dawn of an eternal day. Faith would carry him through the valley, over the hills, beyond the mists, until by grace he would stand in his Lord's presence. Borrowing John's text, Paul could say, "This is the means whereby I triumph—*faith*." God is immeasurably wealthy; His resources know no limitations. His ways, too, are strange; for when a man discovers the bankruptcy of his own virtues, loses his self-confidence, and in despair turns his eyes toward the heavens, then into that man's poverty is poured divine wealth. There is a bankruptcy which is superb—this kind.

Transparent Clothing!

The Bible is a storehouse of scintillating illustrations; often certain Scriptures perfectly describe what is taught elsewhere. The value of righteousness by faith is never seen to better advantage than in the earliest account of man's folly. We are told that when Adam sinned, he became conscious of his nakedness, and with Eve's assistance "sewed fig leaves together, and made themselves aprons" (Gen. 3:7). This was man's first attempt to hide his shame. That he succeeded in a primitive fashion, none could deny; *at least he was no longer naked.* "And they heard the voice of the Lord God walking in the garden in the cool of the day: and Adam and his wife hid themselves from the presence of the Lord God amongst the trees of the garden. And the Lord God called unto Adam, and said unto him, Where art thou? And he said, I heard thy voice in the garden, and I was afraid, *because I was naked*; and I hid myself" (vv. 8-10).

But surely, Adam made a mistake! *He had been naked,* but now was clothed. That is precisely what Adam believed, until the voice of God shattered his complacency. Then he knew he was still naked. Adam was never adequately clothed until he received from God's hand the coat of skins—a garment obtained through sacrifice. The same truth is revealed in the account of the demoniac of Gadara. It is written, "When Jesus went forth to land, there met him out of the city a certain man, which had devils long time, *and ware no clothes,* neither abode in any house, but in the tombs" (Luke 8:27). Probably the man resisted all efforts to clothe him; he saw no need of garments, and was perfectly content to remain naked. Yet when the Saviour delivered him, his eyes were opened and he accepted the garment which either Christ or a disciple offered. "Then the people went out to see what was done; and came to Jesus, and found the man, out of whom the devils were departed, sitting at the feet of Jesus, *clothed,* and in his right mind: and they were afraid" (v. 35). The Word of God states that our best righteousness is as filthy rags; our most efficient efforts cannot hide the nakedness of the soul. We need to be clothed with righteousness which is of God by faith (Phil. 3:9).

The Wheel Came Off the Milkcart

George Müller, the founder of the Bristol Orphanage, was a man of great faith. Many stories of his spiritual exploits have been told, but one of the most thrilling related to a milkman. George Müller was in urgent need one morning, for he had no milk to feed his orphans. He was actually praying about the matter when a knock at the door commanded attention. The milkman had lost a wheel from his cart, and was wondering what could be done with the milk. "Could you use it, sir?" The man of prayer smiled. Faith had taken him another step along the path of victorious living.

My Father's Pigeons

The former chapter closed with a triumphant note. Faith carried Paul to his mansion in the sky. Faith enabled him to write, " For I am now ready to be offered, and the time of my *departure* is at hand." (The Greek word *analuseo*, which has been translated " departure," is most interesting, for it expresses two thoughts: *to be set free;* and *to go on a journey.*

Many years ago, my father trained racing pigeons, and in due course reduced the business to a fine art. He would so arrange his preparation that on the eve of an important race, his best bird sat with two fluffy babies. I often wondered why he decided to race that particular bird. Ultimately her basket, with many others, would reach the starting point of the race, far away in northern England or Scotland; and if one could have read the mind of the pigeon, two thoughts would have been detected. *I want my freedom; I want to fly away.* The call of motherhood had stirred her breast, and she longed to respond. Similarly Paul felt he was imprisoned within a basket of flesh. Yet he knew the lid would soon be raised, and instantly he was free he would begin his journey home. " Henceforth there is laid up for me a crown of righteousness, which the Lord . . . shall give me . . . "

Perhaps the same thought might be expressed in the case of a balloon moored to earth. Within the circular canvas is an urge, endeavouring to send the balloon toward the sky. Alas, the restraining ropes of circumstance prevent the realisation of this ambition. Yet when the rope is severed, when freedom has been gained, earth immediately begins to recede. Paul's soul was somewhat like the balloon; but as the moment of liberation approached, exultantly he cried, " O death, where is thy sting? O grave, where is thy victory?" (1 Cor. 15:55). Faith is the key to the divine treasuries. No man can be really poor if he knows how to use it!

The Supreme Need of the Modern Church

Something has gone wrong with our type of Christianity. The church possesses the greatest organisations in the world; controls, directly or indirectly, vast sums of money; has representatives in almost every country, and may draw on enormous reserves of youthful vigour, yet in some strange way remains partially paralysed.

This statement may be devastating, but after much reflection I stress again what I have written. Christian enterprise on foreign fields seems to be progressing; new institutions in the homelands are on the increase. Even the shortest journey through the countryside supplies evidence that old church buildings are disappearing, and in their place ornate sanctuaries are lifting costly steeples toward the sky. There is a realm in which the church is advancing, but something seems to have gone wrong. Often the services are most attractive; the quality of the singing is better than ever before; the ministers are cultured men of eminence enjoying the respect of the community; the offerings, increasing year after year, run into millions of dollars. Certain people are filled with ecstacy, for the continuance of Christianity is assured; but it is probable that if an old prophet suddenly reappeared to investigate our spiritual assets, he would frown. Our ecclesiastical machinery is of the best quality, but the power to drive it is diminishing.

The church is suffering from an old complaint—Lockjaw. We denounce the activities and doctrines of various sects, but the fact remains that the untiring Jehovah's Witnesses put us to shame. We denounce their teachings, we criticise their endeavours; but how many of our nominal church members would be willing and anxious, week after week, to stand on a street corner offering Christianity to uninterested people? Evangelism, for the normal church, is something exclusively linked with the coming of a special missioner. In preparation for his meetings certain visits might be made, and various people asked to attend the forthcoming crusade. The interest might extend beyond the stipulated time of the evangelist's stay, but afterward the tendency is for all to slump back into complacent indifference. The greatest spiritual need of present times is for a resurgence of that spiritual passion which enables Christians to witness for the Master.

The best way to witness for Christ is to do it! In my travels around the world I have often been asked, "What is the best way to witness for Christ? How may I win my friends for the Saviour? I want to do this, but I'm no speaker." Let me confess that sometimes my patience has been strained when the questioner waxes eloquent in explaining his inability to speak! The statement, "I would not know what to say" provided a striking contrast to the rich smooth flow of breath-taking arguments which cascaded from resolute lips.

Let us face the fact instantly that the Lord Jesus Christ expects every Christian to be a witness, and unless we endeavour to become this, we disappoint Him. There can never be any line of demarcation in this matter. The influential business executive, the typist, the professor, the student, the doctor, the nurse, the husband, the housewife; from the oldest to the youngest; deacons, Sunday-school scholars—*all who profess allegiance to Christ must be witnesses.* The tragedy of the modern church is that a pseudo-dignity has given us lockjaw!

If certain church elders who are business managers stood up in the directors' meeting to say, "Gentlemen, I want you to listen while I tell you what Christ means to me," the audience would swoon, the Stock Exchange would stampede, the Government would be overthrown, and the top slide off Mount Everest! These things are just not done; no sir!

Drinkers mix soda water with their whiskey because they value the linings of their stomachs; some witnesses dilute their message because they value popularity with their friends. The ancient prophets began with, "Thus saith the Lord"; their modern counterparts often question how "this will go over with Mr. So-and-so." Consequently, empty pews have spread like an epidemic of measles. In numerous lands students have repeatedly asked, "How best can I witness for Christ?" My answer has always been, *witness.* When I have been asked, "How may I make my witnessing more effective?" I assumed the inquirer was already on the job. There are certain clearly defined laws in the art of soul-winning.

My life must be more eloquent than my tongue

A man may be a most accomplished orator, a born actor, an excellent exponent of rhetoric, but if his inconsistent life contradicts his words, he becomes a windbag whose exertions merely make nostrils quiver in disgust. Holiness is the handmaiden of all true preaching.

My speech must be simple, attractive, and direct

From time immemorial God has used "the foolishness of preaching," but that fact does not provide a licence for anything slipshod, ungracious, or unthoughtful. I have known speakers who failed to differentiate between brutal arrogance and forthright sincerity. Their atomic denunciations revealed they would have been ideal companions for a blacksmith's hammer. I have known others whose whispered apologies declared them to be excellent baby sitters! Whether I be a minister of a church, a manager in an office, a typist, or errand boy, my confession of Christ should be sincere, convincing, and completely attractive. Listeners should recognise that Christ means more than any tongue could possibly tell.

As far as possible, I should devote sufficient time to the preparation of my message

The man who has completely mastered the art of preaching should be playing a harp! The minister who knows everything should have a call—to another world. Men who glibly say, " I have no need to prepare a sermon, for the moment I open my mouth, God fills it," have either too small a brain or too large a mouth! It is an indisputable fact that God honours preparation. Satan so fears real preaching that he will run a man off his feet doing all sorts of odd jobs, so that the Sunday sermons will be a few sandwiches hastily thrown together instead of a substantial meal for God's hungry children. No man has a right to stand in the pulpit until his own soul has been thrilled by the message to be delivered. And in similar fashion, even an office boy may intelligently plan his approach to friends.

I must beware of moments of success

At such times I shall be in real danger. If, on the other hand, I feel a failure, I can find consolation in the fact that that there will be another time! I must determine to succeed. My own experience has taught that oftentimes God has been able to accomplish far more when I felt a failure than when I felt I had been a great success. We must always remember that the less room we take in the picture, the more God can claim for Himself.

Reader, could *you* effectively witness for Christ? Certainly. Plan your campaign in your daily sphere of service; prepare the way by believing prayer, and then *witness*. If your blood pressure rises, if your knees seem to knock together, if your head swirls, if you feel like nothing on earth, find comfort in the fact that you belong to a great family. These are the initiation ceremonies to the ranks of the great.